THE WATERGATE SCANDAL

IN UNITED STATES HISTORY

IN
UNITED STATES
HISTORY

★ DAVID K. FREMON ★

Enslow Publishers, Inc.
40 Industrial Road
Box 398
Berkeley Heights, NJ 07922
USA
http://www.enslow.com

Dedicated to the memory of Tommy Pacana

Library of Congress Cataloging-in-Publication Data

Fremon, David K.
    [Watergate scandal in American history]
    The Watergate scandal in United States history / David K. Fremon.
    pages cm. — (In United States history)
    Original edition published under title: Watergate scandal in American history. Springfield, NJ : Enslow, 1998.
    Includes bibliographical references and index. ISBN 978-0-7660-6107-1
    1. Watergate Affair, 1972–1974 —Juvenile literature. 2. Nixon, Richard M. (Richard Milhous), 1913–1994 —Juvenile literature. 3. United States— Politics and government—1969–1974
    —Juvenile literature. I. Title. E860.F74 2014
    973.924092—dc 3

                2014000572

Future Editions:
Paperback ISBN: 978-0-7660-6108-8
EPUB: 978-0-7660-6109-5
Single-User PDF ISBN: 978-0-7660-6110-1
Multi-User PDF ISBN: 978-0-7660-6111-8

Printed in the United States of America
072014 HF Group, North Manchester, IN
10 9 8 7 6 5 4 3 2

To Our Readers: We have done our best to make sure all Internet addresses in this book were active and appropriate when we went to press. However, the author and the publisher have no control over and assume no liability for the material available on those Internet sites or on other Web sites they may link to. Comments can be sent by e-mail to comments@enslow.com or to the address on the back cover.

Illustration Credits: Enslow Publishers, Inc., p. 19; Library of Congress, pp. 1, 4.

Cover Illustration: Library of Congress

☆ CONTENTS ☆

The official White House portrait of Richard Milhous Nixon.

Chapter 1

"A THIRD-RATE BURGLARY ATTEMPT"

Frank Wills quietly made his rounds at the Watergate hotel-office complex in Washington, D.C. So far the security guard had spotted nothing unusual. June 17, 1972, promised to be a night like any other.

Then Wills saw a piece of tape being used to hold a garage door open. Perhaps some late-night worker put it there and forgot to remove it. Wills took off the tape and continued his inspection. An hour later he returned. Someone had re-taped the door. Wills alerted a supervisor. The supervisor called the police shortly before 2 A.M.

Six stories above Wills, other people were hard at work. Bernard Barker, a Cuban exile living in Miami, was taking photographs of documents at the Democratic National Committee headquarters. He was aided by two other exiles, Eugenio Martinez and Virgilio Gonzalez, and an American soldier of fortune named Frank Sturgis. With them was a former Central Intelligence Agency (CIA) agent named James McCord. He placed a wiretap on the telephone of the Democratic Party Chairman Lawrence O'Brien.

In a hotel room in the same building, E. Howard Hunt and G. Gordon Liddy waited. They had employed the four Miamians to help find information that could be damaging to the Democrats and help reelect President Richard M. Nixon. Three weeks earlier McCord had bungled a wiretap attempt. The men were in the hotel this night to repair damage and secure more data.

They were hardly professional burglars. McCord supplied walkie-talkies for the team. Two were discarded when the batteries did not work. Hunt and Liddy took one of the radio devices. Another went to Alfred Baldwin, a lookout posted in a hotel room across the street. Barker kept one walkie-talkie. The static from Barker's machine irritated his fellow spies. Someone told him to turn off the walkie-talkie, so Barker did.

At the same time, a carload of plainclothes police approached the building. Since they were driving an unmarked car, Baldwin failed to notice them. The cops made their way to an eighth-floor office, in which a burglary had been reported a few days earlier.

When they turned on the lights, Baldwin responded. He called to Liddy, "Are any of your guys wearing hippie clothes?"

"Negative," Liddy responded. "Our guys are in business suits. Why? Over."

Baldwin replied, "There's four, maybe five guys running around the sixth floor. Lights are going on. One's wearing a cowboy hat, another a sweatshirt. Oh, oh, they've got guns. Looks like trouble."[1]

Liddy frantically tried to call Barker. Close the operation! Get out of there quick! Barker did not reply. He could not hear Liddy's screams, because he had turned off his walkie-talkie.

"Sturgis quickly came in, and we saw a light go on behind him," McCord later recalled. "He told us the obvious—someone had come in the back door, and that 'someone' was law enforcement personnel. We immediately heard them searching rooms at the other end of the wing, shouting 'Come out, police' . . . After a momentary pause, we stood up, arms in the air."[2] Barker turned on his radio and sent a simple message: "They got us."[3]

No one at the time could imagine the consequences of this break-in. Ron Ziegler, Nixon's press secretary, called it a "third-rate burglary attempt."[4] Yet the arrests led to the discovery of one illegal act after another. Less than two years after winning re-election with one of the biggest landslides in history, Richard Nixon would resign in disgrace—because of the scandal known as Watergate.

"I HAD TO WIN"

Whittier was a small town outside Los Angeles when Richard Milhous Nixon was born there in 1913. His father Frank was a fruit farmer who also owned a small store. His mother Hannah raised five sons.

Other boys played; Richard Nixon worked. Most days he woke before dawn, drove crops into Los Angeles, then returned to study, work some more, and sleep. Even as a child he was serious. His mother made him wear starched shirts to school every day. She also insisted that teachers call him "Richard," not "Dick" or "Rick."

Young Nixon's hard work paid off. He won a scholarship to nearby Whittier College. He gained a reputation as a master debater, good musician, and mediocre football player. Although never popular, he was elected student body president of the college. Nixon promised to persuade the school administration to allow dances on campus. He kept that promise.

Nixon went to Duke University Law School, where his serious attitude earned him the nickname "Gloomy Gus."[1] He finished third in his class, but the standing brought little glory. Instead of getting a high-prestige job with the Federal Bureau of Investigation (FBI) or a top New York City law firm, he returned to Whittier and joined a law firm there.

Richard Nixon's persistence even showed in his social life. Thelma "Pat" Ryan was a popular young woman. Young Richard was so impressed by her that he even drove her to her dates with other men. She finally agreed to marry him.

Nixon was exempt from military service because his Quaker religion practiced pacifism. However, he enlisted in the Navy during World War II. Nixon spent most of the war on a small Pacific island, running a supply depot. It was hardly a thrilling assignment, but it proved to be a profitable one. He learned to play poker and ended the war with thousands of dollars in winnings. That money immediately proved useful.

"Tricky Dick"

An unusual want ad ran in several southern California newspapers in early 1946. It sought "Any young man resident of the district, preferably a veteran, fair education" to run for Congress against Democrat Jerry Voorhis.[2] A group of Republican businessmen called the Committee of One Hundred sponsored the ad.

Whittier banker Herman Perry advised Nixon of the notice. Nixon sought the committee's support, and the members gave it to him. Perry predicted, "If you boys ever want to sleep in the White House, get on this Nixon bandwagon."[3] Another Republican called Nixon "the best of a bad lot."[4] The choice of candidate seemed to make little difference, however, because Jerry Voorhis was a popular incumbent.

Nixon conceded nothing. He tore into Voorhis with incredible ferocity. The result was an extremely dirty campaign against the Democrat.

The United States and its allies had just defeated Germany and Japan. Now a new powerful enemy arose. The Soviet Union (Russia and its neighboring "republics") had overrun Eastern European nations during the war. Millions of Americans feared that the communist power sought to take away their property and enslave them as well.

Nixon played upon this fear. During the candidates' first debate, Nixon claimed that a group falsely accused of communist ties supported the Democrat. He kept Voorhis on the defensive for the rest of the campaign. "Of course I knew Jerry Voorhis wasn't a communist," he admitted later, "but I had to win."[5] He got help from the newspapers. The *Los Angeles Times* refused to print anything about Voorhis, while giving Nixon favorable coverage. Nixon won by sixteen thousand votes.

Freshman Congressman Richard Nixon was assigned to the House Committee on Un-American Activities (HUAC). The HUAC was perhaps the most controversial committee in Congress. Its friends claimed it helped protect the nation from communists and other threats. Its foes claimed it went on "witch hunts" and violated people's civil rights.

In 1947 the HUAC held hearings on communists in the United States government. One of the people who testified was Whittaker Chambers, an admitted former communist. The poorly-dressed Chambers hardly made a good impression. "Everything about him looked wrinkled and unpressed," Nixon later recalled.[6]

Chambers named several former communists in the government. One of them was Alger Hiss, director of the Carnegie Endowment for International Peace. Tall, dapper Hiss appeared before the committee. He denied all charges. He said he did not know Chambers. Most of the committee members were willing to ignore Chambers's charge, but not Richard Nixon. Through dogged questioning, Nixon got Hiss to admit that he knew Chambers.

Later, Chambers led reporters to a pumpkin patch near his house. He reached inside a hollowed-out pumpkin and pulled out rolls of microfilm. They contained documents that former State Department employee Hiss had passed on to him during their communist days. The typing on the "pumpkin papers" matched that of Hiss's wife's typewriter. Chambers proved that Alger Hiss was a former communist spy. Richard Nixon, because of his persistence in the case, became the most famous congressman in the nation.

Some questioned whether Nixon's pursuit of Hiss stemmed from true opposition to communism. HUAC Chief Investigator Robert Stripling claimed "Nixon had his hat set for Hiss. He was no more concerned whether Hiss was a [communist] or a billygoat."[7] It made no difference. Nixon played his fame into a 1950 race for the United States Senate.

Congresswoman and former actress Helen Gahagan Douglas was his opponent. Nixon tried the same tactics against her that worked against Voorhis. Nixon spoke against the "red" (communist) menace. He had no more proof that she was a communist than he had that Voorhis was. Nevertheless, he called her the "pink lady" and claimed she was "pink right down to her underwear." Nixon forces circulated the "pink sheet."[8] This brochure, on pink paper, listed Douglas votes that coincided with those of a New York congressman believed to be a communist sympathizer. Douglas was not universally popular among Democrats, and Nixon worked for Democratic support. He won the election easily.

Not everyone approved of Nixon's methods. A writer from the *Independent Review* gave him a name that stuck—"Tricky Dick."[9] The criticism made little difference. Richard Nixon was not climbing the political ladder; he was leaping up it.

The "Checkers" Speech

In 1952 Democrats had served as presidents for twenty years. Even so, the party appeared vulnerable. General Dwight D. "Ike" Eisenhower, commander of the World War II D-Day invasion of Europe, was the Republican candidate. For many the choice appeared obvious. How could anyone vote against the man who had saved the free world?

Republicans needed a running mate for the popular former general. Eisenhower himself showed little interest in politics. Republican leaders, seeking to "balance the ticket," chose Nixon to run with him. "Ike" was old; Nixon was young. Ike was an easterner, then living in New York City; Nixon was a Californian. Eisenhower's political views were moderate; Nixon's were more conservative. Republicans hoped these opposites would attract as many votes as possible.

The campaign rolled smoothly until mid-September. Then on September 18, *The New York Times* ran a headline that read "Secret Nixon Fund." The paper's story said that a group of California businessmen had donated more than $18,000 to pay for Nixon's campaign expenses.

There was nothing secret or illegal about this fund. Several other politicians, including Democratic presidential candidate Adlai Stevenson, had such funds. Yet Eisenhower, who had attacked Democratic corruption throughout the campaign, did not want a hint of scandal. He refused to speak on behalf of his running mate. Pressure mounted for Nixon to resign from the ticket.

He refused to do so. Instead, he arranged for a half-hour television program to explain the fund. Fifty-eight million viewers, the largest television audience in history to that time, tuned in to see what he would say. "This broadcast must not be just good. It must be a smash hit," Nixon said.[10]

Nixon waded through every detail of his finances. He accounted for every penny. He said his family was not rich. He told viewers that his wife Pat "doesn't have a mink coat, but she does have a respectable Republican cloth coat."[11] He concluded by saying that a contributor gave their family a cocker spaniel puppy named Checkers, "and regardless of what they say about it, we're going to keep it."[12] Nixon urged viewers to phone or telegraph the Republican National Committee to let the committee know if he should stay on the ticket.

Nixon liked to refer to it as the Fund Speech. Almost everyone else remembered it as the Checkers Speech. Either way, the response was overwhelming. Thousands of cards, letters, and telegrams poured in, praising the wholesome Nixon family. Eisenhower might not have wanted Nixon as a partner, but now he had no choice. "You're my boy," he proclaimed.[13] Eisenhower and Nixon won by a landslide in 1952.

Vice President Nixon

Few vice presidents were busier in office than Richard Nixon. He traveled around the country and the world. He campaigned in 1954 on behalf of Republican candidates. Yet in 1956 Eisenhower wanted to dump Nixon as his running mate.[14] He offered the still-young Nixon any office in the Cabinet except secretary of state. Nixon refused. If he were to step down, someone else would be next in line for the presidency.

Eisenhower's second term proved adventurous. Heart attacks and bowel illnesses troubled the elderly president. Nixon served as acting president while Eisenhower was hospitalized. He handled the responsibilities well. A 1958 goodwill trip to South America nearly ended in tragedy. A mob attacked Nixon's car in Caracas, Venezuela. The vice president and his party barely escaped with their lives. During a 1959 visit to the Soviet Union, Nixon and Soviet Premier Nikita Khrushchev engaged in a shouting match. Both raised their voices at each other, but each claimed it was a friendly discussion.

The Great Debate

John F. Kennedy, a young senator from Massachusetts, won heated primary elections and the 1960 Democratic presidential nomination. Lyndon Johnson, the powerful Senate leader from the state of Texas, accepted the vice-presidential nomination. Richard Nixon won unanimous approval at the Republican convention.

This began one of the most spirited and energetic campaigns in American history. Kennedy and Nixon drew up nonstop schedules. Nixon promised to visit all fifty states. A late August knee injury made Nixon's vow seem foolish. The Republican spent two weeks in the hospital.

The still-popular Eisenhower offered little help. A reporter asked him to name a major contribution Nixon had made to his presidency. Ike replied, "If you give me a week, I'll think of one."[15]

Although trailing in the polls, Nixon felt confident. The candidates had agreed to a series of televised debates. Advisors told him the debates were a bad idea, because they would give the lesser-known Kennedy publicity. Yet Nixon knew he was an excellent debater, and the Checkers Speech had shown he could do well on television.

John Kennedy relaxed on September 26. He sunned himself on the roof of his Chicago hotel. Nixon, meanwhile, kept up a frantic schedule of appearances. He re-injured his knee. Just before the debate, Kennedy strolled into the television studio. Nixon limped into it.

What the candidates debated was not memorable, but the unusual results were. Most who listened to the debate on the radio thought Nixon came out ahead. Those who saw it on television gave a different story.

Kennedy looked young and tanned. "I have never seen him looking more fit," Nixon recalled.[16] Those who saw Nixon saw something else. The Republican winced from his knee problem. He looked pale and haggard. After the debate, his mother asked if he was ill.

By election day it was too close to call. When election night ended, the outcome was still uncertain. Kennedy finally won by only 119,000 votes out of more than 69 million votes cast. He took 303 electoral votes to Nixon's 219.

Republicans claimed election irregularities in Illinois, Texas, and Missouri. If electoral votes from these states went to Nixon, the total would give him the election. Nixon refused to contest the states. "[He] decided it would disrupt the country too much were he to contest," said aide Herb Klein. "It would take a long time, and leave the country in turmoil."[17]

After the election Nixon wrote a political autobiography titled *Six Crises*. There would be many more crises in his future.

"You Won't Have Nixon"

Two years later Richard Nixon ran for governor of California. The campaign itself was less historic than what happened when he lost on election night.

At first, defeated candidate Nixon declined to answer questions. Finally he met reporters. "I have no complaints about the press coverage," he said. "I have never complained about it."[18] Then he proceeded to complain about how the press had covered the election. For more than fifteen minutes, he rambled on about politics, unfair coverage of him by the media, and anything else. Some reporters thought they were watching a nervous breakdown take place before their eyes.[19]

Nixon concluded:

One last thing . . . For years you've had a lot of fun . . . You've had the opportunity to attack me. . . . Just think how much you're going to be missing. You won't have

Nixon to kick around anymore because, gentlemen, this is my last press conference.[20]

Nixon Returns

Nixon and his family moved to New York City in 1963. There he met a prosperous attorney named John Mitchell. He and Mitchell became friends, and Nixon took a job at Mitchell's law firm. For the first time in his life, Richard Nixon was becoming wealthy.

In 1964 Nixon campaigned for Republican presidential nominee Barry Goldwater. Two years later he spoke throughout the country to support Republican political candidates. Hundreds, if not thousands, of Republican officeholders owed him favors. In 1968 he called in those favors. Nixon beat two opponents for the Republican presidential nomination. Then he sat back and watched the Democrats destroy themselves.

President Richard Nixon

For nearly a generation the Vietnam War had split the nation. France had colonized the Southeast Asian country, but communist-backed rebels ousted them. A 1954 treaty gave communists the northern half of the country, while an American-backed government held the south. Both sides wanted full control of the country. They fought a civil war for that rule.

American involvement in the war grew. President Kennedy sent "advisors" (actually military troops) to Vietnam. When Lyndon Johnson became president following Kennedy's 1963 assassination, the war expanded. In 1964, after communist forces supposedly sank U.S.

ships in the Gulf of Tonkin, Johnson got congressional approval to build up the war.

By 1968 the communist-backed North Vietnamese were advancing into the south. What would the United States do? Some Americans favored all-out military force to destroy the North Vietnamese. Yet as American casualties grew, an increasing number favored withdrawing all troops.

Johnson, stung by antiwar criticism, decided not to seek re-election. Only one Democrat, Senator Robert F. Kennedy, brother of the late president, might have received support from both pro-war "hawks" and antiwar "doves." However, an assassin had killed him on June 5. The Democratic nomination was up for grabs.

Tempers escalated inside Chicago's International Amphitheater as the Democratic National Convention wore on. Outside, things were worse. Police clashed daily with antiwar demonstrators. On the Wednesday of the convention, officers beat and arrested hundreds of people. Some of those arrested were violence-prone radicals. Others were innocent passersby.

Nixon might have thought the chaotic convention assured his election. It did not. Hubert Humphrey, Johnson's vice president, won the Democratic nomination. At first he supported Johnson's war policies, and his campaign went nowhere. In late September, however, Humphrey changed his stance. He started opposing the war, and Democratic support came back to him.

Republicans who had thought they could breeze through election day now had to sweat through it. Former Alabama Governor George Wallace ran as an independent and put up a challenge in the South. Nixon won, but by only seven hundred thousand votes over Humphrey.

Nixon worked hard his first term. He concentrated on his favorite field, foreign policy. He reduced the number of American soldiers stationed in Vietnam. Under his "Vietnamization" program, South Vietnamese troops would be prepared to fight their own war. While continuing the Vietnam War, he negotiated with the two communist superpowers. Nixon moved to establish diplomatic relations with mainland China. He also signed a nuclear arms reduction treaty with the Soviet Union.

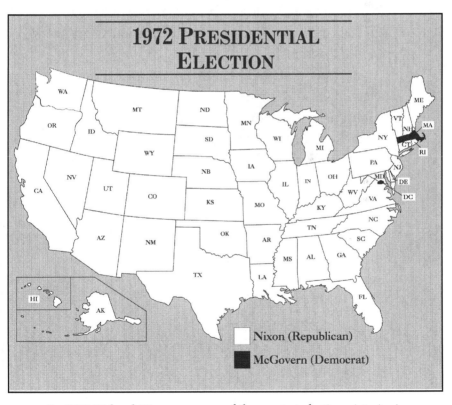

In 1972 Richard Nixon won one of the greatest election victories in American history. Democratic candidate George McGovern won a majority of votes only in Massachusetts and the District of Columbia.

The Democrats continued their chaos in 1972. South Dakota Senator George McGovern, a man disliked by many party professionals, won the nomination. For a running mate he chose Missouri Senator Thomas Eagleton. A few days later media reported that while hospitalized for depression, Eagleton had received electric shock treatments. It sounded horrible to many Americans. They questioned Eagleton's ability to face the pressures of high office. They also questioned McGovern's judgment in choosing him. Eagleton, under pressure from McGovern, resigned from the ticket.

Nixon won re-election by a huge margin. McGovern out-polled the Republican only in Massachusetts and the District of Columbia.

That election night in 1972 should have been the happiest night of Richard Nixon's life. After all, he had triumphed with one of the greatest landslides in American history. Instead of smiling, though, Richard Nixon fretted. He had problems on his mind—problems that would destroy his presidency less than two years later.

Chapter 3

"WHITE HOUSE HORRORS"

Americans knew of the Watergate break-in when they cast their votes for president in November 1972. It seemed to make little difference. Perhaps they would have felt differently if they knew all the facts. In the coming months they would learn of other illegal acts—what Nixon Campaign Manager John Mitchell referred to as "White House horrors."[1]

Plugging Leaks

Richard Nixon inherited the Vietnam War. He wanted to remove the United States from it. There were three ways to leave Vietnam. He could go all out and order the destruction of North Vietnam, but few Americans desired this kind of war. He could withdraw all troops immediately, but Nixon was afraid such a move would look like a sign of weakness to the communist superpowers. Or he could train and arm the South Vietnamese army while gradually withdrawing United States troops. Nixon chose the third option.

The plan involved bombing Vietcong (communist) bases in South Vietnam. Neighboring Cambodia, although officially neutral, also harbored Vietcong bases. Nixon ordered those bombed. Word of the Cambodian bombings reached the American press. *The New York Times* printed stories denouncing the bombings.

Nixon was furious. Someone in his administration was "leaking" information to the press. This information, he claimed, could cost American lives and disrupt national security. He ordered the FBI to place wiretaps on the phones of thirteen government officials and four prominent reporters.

These wiretaps did little to halt antiwar protests. Thousands gathered in Washington, D.C., in late 1969. More than four hundred colleges and universities had demonstrations against the war. In May 1970 at Ohio's Kent State University, the governor called out the National Guard. Instead of keeping the peace, panicking guardsmen shot at the crowd. Four students died, and several more were injured.

Like many Americans, Nixon feared antiwar protests were communist-inspired. His theory, however, received no support from the nation's intelligence agencies. FBI Director J. Edgar Hoover refused to help Nixon gather information on antiwar leaders. The CIA investigated the matter. It found no links between communists and opponents of the war. The Internal Revenue Service (IRS) refused to investigate the tax-exempt status of antiwar groups.

A former U.S. Army intelligence officer named Tom Charles Huston proposed a domestic spy network. Nixon discussed the Huston plan with heads of the nation's security agencies. Hoover thought the plan was a terrible idea.

Unhappy with the government agencies, Nixon decided to start his own intelligence-gathering force. This unit would be composed of White House (presidential) staff and would answer only to the president. Domestic Advisor John Ehrlichman would head this top secret outfit. Egil "Bud" Krogh and David Young assisted him. The unit became known as the "Plumbers," because their job was to fix security leaks. The Plumbers did not have to wait long for an assignment.

Plumbers

A *New York Times* story on June 13, 1971, startled the nation. "Vietnam Archive Study Traces 3 Decades of Growing U.S. Involvement," the headline declared. Other stories followed. The published documents, which made public a secret study of the war, became known as the Pentagon Papers.

These papers described presidential administrations earlier than Nixon's. Nonetheless, the president raged. These papers were top secret. Release of them should be considered treason. The government sued to stop the publication of the Pentagon Papers. The Supreme Court, however, upheld the right of the *Times* and other newspapers to print them.

Failing to stop the publication of the papers, the White House could at least attack their leaker. Daniel Ellsberg, a former official in Lyndon Johnson's administration, at one time supported the war. When he changed his mind, he collected the documents, then turned them over to the press.

Nixon's administration sought to get back at Ellsberg. He was indicted and charged with unauthorized possession of national defense information and the theft of government property. Legal retaliation was not enough. Nixon also wanted to discredit Ellsberg.[2]

The FBI would be no help. Director Hoover was a friend of Ellsberg's father-in-law. The CIA wrote a psychological profile on Ellsberg. "There is no suggestion that the subject saw anything treasonous in his act," the report read. "Rather, he seemed to be responding to what he deemed a higher level of patriotism."[3] This was not exactly the kind of incriminating report the "Plumbers" wanted.

Ehrlichman and the other Plumbers realized they would have to gather their own information. There seemed to be an easy solution. Ellsberg was seeing a psychiatrist, Dr. Lewis Fielding. An "unannounced" visit to Fielding's office might produce some interesting information.

Nixon advisor Charles Colson, who once said he would "walk over my grandmother" for the president, knew the man to head the break-in.[4] Ex-CIA agent E. Howard Hunt had worked on the 1961 Bay of Pigs mission. The botched revolution attempt failed to topple Cuban dictator Fidel Castro, but it made Hunt a hero in Miami's anti-Castro Cuban community. Hunt signed on with the White House staff as a $100 per day consultant.

The Plumbers picked up another colorful recruit. G. Gordon Liddy, as a lawyer, once fired a blank pistol in court to impress a jury. He disciplined himself by holding his hand over a candle even after the flesh burned. Liddy was willing to engage in illegal activities to stop those opposing the administration. "As far as I was concerned, anything went," he said.[5]

Hunt also recruited a Bay of Pigs partner, Bernard Barker. Miami real estate agent Barker then enlisted fellow Cuban exiles Eugenio Martinez and Felipe de Diego. Hunt hinted that if the Cubans helped him with the break-in, he could get government support for a revolution to topple Castro.

Liddy and Hunt flew to Los Angeles in late August 1971. They looked over Fielding's office building. A break-in should be easy. A week later Barker and Diego, disguised as deliverymen, entered the psychiatrist's office. They found nothing. Ehrlichman was unimpressed by the failed mission. He ordered it scrapped.

CRP

Vietnam was not the only worry of the White House in late 1971. Another major concern was the 1972 election. Richard Nixon appeared to face stiff opposition. He must be re-elected—at all costs.

Nixon set up a re-election campaign committee called the Committee to Re-Elect the President (CRP). Foes called the committee "CREEP." The name well described the nature of the campaign.

The White House staff loaned members to the campaign staff. There was little distinction between the two groups. H. R. "Bob" Haldeman ran Nixon's staff with an iron hand. A former colleague described Haldeman as "a completely obnoxious man who was totally uninterested in what anyone else thought."[6] He and Ehrlichman controlled all access to the president. Mitchell, now United States attorney general, doubled as a presidential campaign advisor. A young attorney, John Wesley Dean III, served as special counsel (advisor) to the president. Jeb Stuart Magruder, who was formerly a White House staffer under Haldeman, headed the CRP.

Nobody claimed that the Nixon group was a happy squad. Mitchell loathed Ehrlichman. Communications Director Herb Klein called Colson "one of the meanest people I ever knew."[7] Magruder thought Liddy was unstable and wanted him fired. Gordon Strachan, a CRP deputy, reassured Magruder by saying, "Liddy may be a Hitler, but at least he's our Hitler."[8]

Money, Money, Money

Money is the lifeblood of politics. Without it, few campaigns go anywhere. Richard Nixon's team made sure that his campaign would not be short of funds.

The Democrat-controlled Congress passed an election reform bill in early 1972. Nixon signed it, and the bill became law. The previous law required campaigns to list contributors only for general elections. The new law demanded equal disclosures for party primary elections as well. The old law expired in early March 1972. The new one took over on April 7. That left a month for the CRP to gather limitless amounts of money from donors who could remain anonymous.

Maurice Stans excelled at the art of collecting money. The CRP finance director and former United States commerce secretary knew hundreds of corporate directors on a first-name basis. He was not afraid to request huge sums from them. Some of these businesspeople might have been encouraged by the help they could get from a friendly White House. Others feared revenge if they did not contribute.[9] Stans's fund-raising skills helped the Nixon campaign collect $20 million before the disclosure law went into effect.

White House and CRP staffers shuttled around the country picking up these contributions. One hundred thousand dollars was the standard campaign request. CRP's finance committee was so busy it had to turn down donations of "only" fifty thousand dollars.

G. Gordon Liddy was one of the emergency couriers. He picked up two contributions that did not get cashed until after April 7. One was a set of four checks totaling $89,000. The other was a check for $25,000.

Liddy did not deposit them in the CRP account. Instead, he placed the checks in Bernard Barker's Miami bank and immediately cashed them. If he had known the trouble the checks would cause, he would have torn them up and thrown them away.

Liddy walked out of the bank carrying a wad of one-hundred-dollar bills. Barker's bank, by custom with large cash transactions, recorded the serial numbers of the bills. Instead of "laundered" money that was clean and free from detection, Liddy now carried bills that were easily traceable.

Dirty Tricks

Who would Richard Nixon's 1972 presidential opponent be? The Democrats had several strong choices. Senator Edmund Muskie from Maine had run for vice president with Hubert Humphrey in 1968. People around the country admired his cool dignity. Humphrey was another potential candidate. If he ran, he could be a tough foe. Edward Kennedy, brother of the late president John F.

Kennedy, attracted a legion of followers. Former Alabama Governor George Wallace might do well in the South. If he ran as a third-party candidate, he could draw votes from Nixon. Finally, George McGovern represented the antiwar wing of the party. He might attract young people and radicals, but few other voters. To Richard Nixon and his allies, McGovern was the preferred foe.

How could voters be lured to nominate the weakest candidate? Hunt had a plan to disrupt Edward Kennedy's campaign. He spliced together old CIA cables. The new phony cable claimed that John F. Kennedy had ordered the assassination of South Vietnamese Premier Ngo Dinh Diem. If Catholic voters saw that a Catholic president helped murder a Catholic premier, perhaps they would turn to the Republicans.

Another sabotage campaign helped ruin Muskie. Haldeman had a former college classmate who was capable of dirty tricks. Donald Segretti entered the presidential campaign.

Segretti and his recruits damaged the Muskie campaign in many ways. They stole campaign schedules. In Southern white communities, they called voters at midnight to describe what Muskie would do to help black people. At a Wallace rally, they distributed handbills that supposedly came from Muskie's camp. These handbills proclaimed, "If you liked [German dictator Adolf] Hitler, you'll love Wallace."[10]

Muskie expected a huge win at the New Hampshire presidential primary. Instead, events there destroyed him. The state's largest newspaper printed a letter that accused Muskie of insulting French Canadians. The author of this letter was one of Segretti's tricksters. Muskie got a disappointing vote total in his neighboring state.

In Florida the sabotage continued. Nixon forces circulated a letter accusing Humphrey and Washington Senator Henry Jackson of sexual misconduct. The letter had Muskie's name on it. Three leading Democrats were slandered at once.

In late April, Muskie ended his devastated campaign. Kennedy decided not to run. McGovern, meanwhile, outpolled the other Democrats in the primaries. The Republicans would be getting their wish. The weakest candidate would be the Democratic nominee.

The Republican position appeared even stronger in May. A would-be assassin shot George Wallace, paralyzing him from the waist down. There would be no challenge from the feisty Alabaman. To many observers, Richard Nixon's re-election was solidly in hand.

Gemstone

If Nixon's campaign team could have predicted the primary results, the January 27, 1972, meeting might never have taken place. Mitchell, Dean, and Magruder met. Liddy presented an elaborate proposal.

He called the project Gemstone. It was a multifaceted plan involving a variety of illegal acts. Liddy suggested kidnapping possible protesters demonstrating at the Republican Convention and detaining them in Mexico. Organized crime figures, he said, would be happy to help. Liddy talked about employing prostitutes to compromise Democratic candidates, sabotaging the air conditioning system at the Democratic Convention, and bugging the

Democrats' telephone conversations. Liddy said his plan would cost a million dollars.

"I should have thrown Liddy out the window," Mitchell later remarked. Instead, he merely said it was "not quite what we had in mind."[11]

Liddy came back a week later. His revised plan omitted the Mafia kidnappers and faulty air conditioning. Dean told Haldeman the plan was "incredible, unnecessary, and unwise."[12] Haldeman agreed.

If Mitchell, as he later claimed, rejected the second plan outright, Liddy did not get the message. The former FBI man came back in early April. This time, out went the prostitutes. His new plan concentrated on bugging the Democrats. It would cost a quarter of a million dollars.

Mitchell claimed he told Magruder, "We don't need this. . . . Let's not discuss it any further."[13] However, Liddy said a Haldeman aide called him shortly after the meeting. "He relayed a message from Magruder that 'You've got a "go" on your project,'" Liddy wrote.[14]

Armed at last with money, Liddy set to work. Former CIA agent James McCord worked with the White House as a security consultant. Over Hunt's objections, Liddy enlisted McCord. Hunt called his friends Barker and Martinez. Two other Miamians came along: expert locksmith Virgilio Gonzalez and soldier of fortune Frank Sturgis.

Their target was the Democratic National Committee headquarters, on the sixth floor of the Watergate hotel and office complex. They particularly sought to bug the conversations of Democratic Chairman Lawrence O'Brien. On May 22 McCord set up ex-FBI man Alfred Baldwin in a room in a Howard Johnson hotel across from the

Watergate. From there Baldwin could watch the sixth-floor headquarters and monitor wiretapped telephone calls.

Hunt, Liddy, and the Miamians set out to make the wiretaps on May 22. The break-in attempt failed, because someone was wandering around in the building. The would-be invaders tried again the following night. This time they failed because Gonzalez brought the wrong tools. Hunt sent him back to Miami to get the proper equipment.

The third time proved to be the charm. Barker, Martinez, Gonzalez, Sturgis, and McCord entered the building. The Miamians photographed documents while McCord set the wiretaps.

It was not a completely successful mission. One of McCord's wiretaps did not connect properly. Liddy said Mitchell wanted them to go back and fix the bug. Hunt had reservations, but he went along with his partner.

The Miamians and McCord reentered the Watergate early on June 17. This time they were caught. When captured, McCord asked, "Are you the metropolitan police?"[15] The burglars went quietly.

4 Chapter

"A CANCER GROWING ON THE PRESIDENCY"

Within moments of the arrests, the grounds of the Watergate began to look like a carnival. Squad cars with flashing lights surrounded the complex. Officers scurried all over the place.

E. Howard Hunt and G. Gordon Liddy were too busy to watch the spectacle. Bernard Barker had their hotel room key, and police could be there soon. They had to leave fast.

The two burglary team leaders packed their gear. Hunt told Liddy to go and find himself an alibi. They strolled past unsuspecting police to their cars. Hunt drove a couple of blocks, then walked back to Alfred Baldwin's room in the Howard Johnson.

Hunt called a lawyer to free the burglars. Then he told Baldwin to get out of there. "Does this mean I'm out of a job?" Baldwin asked.[1] The lookout then drove McCord's van, which was loaded with surveillance equipment, to McCord's suburban Virginia home. McCord's wife drove him back to the Howard Johnson, and he drove his own car to his home in Connecticut.

After leaving the hotel, Hunt rushed to his White House office. He stuffed the burglary gear into his safe and removed ten thousand dollars in cash. Then he went home.

Unusual Burglars

The five men at the Democratic headquarters surprised the arresting officers. They were polite, quiet, well-dressed, middle-aged men—hardly typical burglars. They carried burglar tools, but they also had cameras, tear gas canisters, bugging devices, a wig, and radio transmitter/ receivers. A search at the police station revealed something else unusual—the burglars were carrying thirteen one-hundred-dollar bills with consecutive serial numbers. The FBI later traced this money to Barker's bank account. Barker was also carrying a check signed by E. Howard Hunt. A search of their hotel rooms revealed more hundred-dollar bills. Investigators also found address books on Barker and Martinez with a telephone number and "H. H.—White House."

Most unusual was the lawyer. An attorney named Douglas Caddy came to the police station and posted bail for the burglars. Where did this lawyer come from? None of the defendants had called to request one.

In one respect the lawyer arrived too late. James McCord had already identified himself. A policeman in court recognized him as an employee of the Committee to Re-Elect the President. It would be the beginning of the end for the Nixon administration.

First Reactions

A few hours later, at mid-morning on Saturday, Liddy arrived at his office at the Committee to Re-Elect the

President. Staff member Robert Odle saw him carrying a large pile of papers. Liddy asked Odle how to operate the shredding machine, then set to work. Liddy spent the next several hours destroying anything that might cast suspicion on him. He destroyed documents, one-hundred-dollar bills, and even soap wrappers saved from hotels he had visited.

After his shred-a-thon, Liddy called CRP leaders, who were vacationing in California. Magruder was furious at Liddy for bringing CRP employee McCord along on the break-in. He was even more angry at himself for not firing Liddy earlier. Word of the blunder got to recently retired Attorney General John Mitchell. Later that afternoon Mitchell told reporters that McCord and the other people involved in the break-in were not working with CRP approval.

Liddy went to talk to Richard Kleindienst, the new attorney general. Kleindienst was at a country club and did not want to be disturbed. Finally he agreed to listen. Liddy told Kleindienst it was a personal request from John Mitchell to release McCord. Kleindienst refused. He phoned his assistant Henry Petersen to make sure the Watergate burglars received no special favors.

Two FBI agents visited Hunt at his home that Saturday afternoon. He told them he would not speak to them without his lawyer present.

President Richard Nixon spent the weekend at the home of his friend Robert Abplanalp in the Bahamas. He returned to his Key Biscayne, Florida, home on Sunday. Nixon saw a *Miami Herald* story titled "Miamians Held in D.C. Try to Bug Demo Headquarters." The story sounded ridiculous. "I dismissed it as some sort of prank," Nixon wrote in his memoirs.[2]

The Money Trail

Bob Woodward was a young reporter working the metropolitan beat for the *Washington Post*. At first the burglary did not seem like much of a story. His interest picked up when he went to court and heard McCord say he was a security consultant and former CIA member. It definitely peaked when he heard that two of the burglars had address books with the telephone number of a White House employee.

Woodward called Hunt the following Monday morning. No one answered Hunt's phone, but the White House receptionist suggested he try Charles Colson's office. Colson's secretary gave him the number of a public relations office where Hunt worked.

Hunt answered the phone. Woodward asked him why his name might have appeared in the address books of two Watergate burglars. "Good God!" Hunt shouted. He added, "I have no comment," then hung up.[3]

On July 25, *The New York Times* reported that several calls had been made from Barker's phone in Miami to a CRP phone used by Liddy. Carl Bernstein, another young *Post* reporter, decided to investigate these calls. A Miami district attorney had subpoenaed to see the telephone list, demanding a copy of it for the court. Bernstein flew to Florida to examine the list. He also found out from the district attorney that checks for more than one hundred thousand dollars had been deposited and withdrawn from Barker's bank account.

Bernstein saw copies of four checks totaling $89,000 from Mexican lawyer Manuel Ogarrio Dagueirre. There was also a fifth check for $25,000 from someone named Kenneth Dahlberg.

Who was Kenneth Dahlberg? The bank's manager knew him as a part-time Florida resident and director of a bank in nearby Fort Lauderdale. The Fort Lauderdale bank president said he believed Dahlberg headed the Midwestern campaign for Richard Nixon.

Using newspaper files, Woodward located Dahlberg in Minnesota. Dahlberg said the $25,000 was money he collected for Nixon's campaign. He turned the check over to either CRP Finance Chair Maurice Stans or Treasurer Hugh Sloan. The money trail now led from CRP to the burglars.

Over the next year Woodward and Bernstein would write more than two hundred stories on the Watergate burglary and other White House misdeeds. These stories put pressure on all branches of government to pursue their Watergate investigations.

Both crafty reporters used a number of sources for their stories. The most famous was a shadowy character known as Deep Throat. Deep Throat was never quoted and never volunteered information. He would only confirm stories Woodward heard elsewhere. If Woodward cared to speak to this source, he left a red flag in a flowerpot on his balcony window. Deep Throat would then circle a page of a newspaper delivered to Woodward, along with the time they would meet in an underground garage.

"Check every lead," Deep Throat advised Woodward. "It goes all over the map. Not one of the games [operations] was free lance. Every one was tied in."[4] Woodward never revealed Deep Throat's name. Finally in 2005, he was revealed as FBI official W. Mark Felt.

Cover-Up

"No one ever considered that there would not be a cover-up," CRP Deputy Director Jeb Stuart Magruder said later.[5] From the time they heard of the break-in, top White House officials strove to keep themselves and CRP officials from being connected to the crime.

In the days following the break-in, they called or met with one another to sketch their plans. Magruder, CRP Director John Mitchell, Chief of Staff H. R. Haldeman, Domestic Advisor John Ehrlichman, White House Counsel John Dean, Special White House Counsel Charles Colson, CRP Counsel Liddy, Mitchell advisor Frederick LaRue, and Haldeman assistant Gordon Strachan all knew of one or more White House horrors before Watergate. In some cases, they were actively involved in the illegalities.

Even if Nixon knew nothing of the break-in beforehand, he moved to hide it afterward. On June 23, 1972, he discussed the problem with Haldeman. The FBI was already investigating the crime, Haldeman said, "and it goes in some directions we don't want it to go."[6] The chief of staff told Nixon that Barker's money had already been traced to the CRP.

If J. Edgar Hoover were alive, the FBI might have found the Nixon link immediately. However, Hoover had died in May. L. Patrick Gray, a former Navy officer known mainly for his loyalty to Nixon, was chosen temporary FBI director.

Nixon and Haldeman decided to use the CIA to halt the FBI Watergate probe. The two government agencies had a long-standing agreement. If one was working on a project, the other stayed out of the way. Haldeman asked CIA Assistant Director Vernon Walters to tell Gray that

Watergate was part of a CIA project. Walters told Gray, and the FBI leader promised to withdraw from the investigation.

Gray, unknowingly, had already become part of the cover-up. Three days earlier, Ehrlichman and Dean had discussed what to do with the contents of Hunt's safe. It contained some very sensitive materials: the phony Diem cables, material damaging to Senator Edward Kennedy, and a file of papers dealing with Daniel Ellsberg. Ehrlichman suggested that Dean "deep six" the materials—throw them off a bridge into the Potomac River. Dean, instead, decided to give them to acting FBI Director Gray. He told Gray they were potentially dangerous materials that "should never see the light of day," but did not deal with the Watergate break-in.[7] Gray took the folder of papers home and ignored it.

The gullible Gray went along with requests to stay away from Watergate. Yet even he was having suspicions. On July 6 he warned the president that people on his staff "are trying to mortally wound you." He expected a shocked reaction from Nixon. Instead, the president all but told him to go away. "Pat, you just continue your thorough and aggressive investigation," Nixon said.[8]

White House Counsel Dean took responsibility for the cover-up. The five men caught at the Democratic headquarters would obviously be found guilty. Hunt and Liddy (who had been linked to the burglars through Martinez's address book) would also fall. But higher-up White House staff—Mitchell, Magruder, Haldeman, and Ehrlichman—so far remained untouched.

Nixon claimed at an August 29 press conference that no one on the White House staff was involved in the break-in. "What really hurts in matters of this sort is not the fact that they occur because overzealous people in campaigns do things that are wrong," he said. "What really hurts is if you try to cover it up."[9]

In criminal cases, defendants and other witnesses testify before a twenty-three-member grand jury. Then the grand jury decides if there is enough evidence to bring a case to trial. It hands down indictments against people who might be guilty. On September 15 the five burglars, Hunt, and Liddy were indicted. Magruder escaped indictment because he perjured himself (lied to the jury). The trial would not take place until January—well after election day in November.

Nixon congratulated Dean on minimizing damage to the White House. Dean warned that the case might not stay hidden forever.

Hush Money

Already, the cover of Watergate was starting to unravel. John Mitchell resigned as CRP director on July 1. Even though he claimed he never authorized a break-in, it was too dangerous to have him around. Alfred Baldwin, the lookout, quietly turned himself in to the FBI. He would not be prosecuted if he agreed to testify in upcoming court cases.

The burglars had huge lawyer bills and other expenses, which they expected the government to pay. It was their price for remaining silent about the break-in and other crimes.

The price kept rising. E. Howard Hunt's wife, Dorothy, handled the payments for the accused men. At first she demanded $130,000 for legal fees and $59,000 in living expenses for the men. By mid-September the demand grew to $400,000 in expenses. This money came from CRP funds, but even that supply was limited. After the election, it would come from a special fund Haldeman had saved from previous elections.

On December 8, an airplane from Washington crashed near Chicago's Midway Airport. A congressman and a well-respected Chicago reporter were among those killed. Attention, however, fell upon Dorothy Hunt. Her body was found with ten thousand dollars in one-hundred-dollar bills. Why was she carrying so much cash? Even though reporters and investigators had no proof, many suspected that this was "hush money" intended for the burglars.

"Maximum John"

None of the arrested Watergate burglars had a criminal record. Perhaps Nixon thought that a judge would notice their clean pasts and give them light sentences. If so, he was mistaken.

Judge John J. Sirica had been given the nickname Maximum John. He was a no-nonsense judge known for giving stiff sentences to offenders. Sirica believed there was more to this burglary than a handful of people breaking into a building. He intended to find out the truth behind Watergate. Who hired the burglars? Why were they there?

The defendants were not talking. Liddy behaved like a captured soldier, giving only the most basic information. Hunt changed his plea from not guilty to guilty, hoping for a lighter sentence. The four Miamians followed Hunt's lead.

McCord had no intention of spending a single night in jail. He refused to plead guilty. Dean, through former New

York policeman Jack Caulfield, made McCord an offer "from the highest levels of the White House."[10] McCord would get clemency (leniency) and a good job if he pleaded guilty and promised to remain silent. It was no deal. McCord and Liddy were found guilty on January 30, 1973. They were to be sentenced on March 23.

Sirica's Birthday Present

Richard M. Nixon was sworn in to his second term of office in January 1973. Two months later, his presidency was already collapsing. Watergate, which he had dismissed as a prank, was coming back as a nightmare.

Hunt's money demands kept rising. Now he wanted an extra $122,000. Dean met with the president on March 21. "There is a cancer growing on the presidency," he said, talking about the growing hush money totals.[11] If this cancer were not destroyed, it could ruin the presidency. Dean told Nixon it could cost a million dollars to keep the burglars quiet over the next two years. The president said the money could be raised.

James McCord walked into Judge Sirica's chamber on March 19. He handed the judge a sealed envelope. March 20 was Sirica's sixty-ninth birthday. He could not have received a better present.

Three days later, Sirica read McCord's letter in court. McCord claimed there was political pressure on the Watergate defendants to remain silent. Other individuals were identified. McCord claimed there had been massive perjury during the trial—many people had lied before the court. He also said that the break-in was not a CIA operation, although the Miamians might have been told so.

Judge Sirica handed out the sentences. They were stiffer than anyone had imagined. Liddy got six years and eight months to twenty years in prison, as well as a $40,000 fine. The Miamians each received forty years. Hunt got thirty years. The judge said he might change the sentences if the defendants cooperated with the upcoming Senate Watergate Committee.

Sirica blamed the prosecutors for handling the case poorly. Seven men were convicted. Yet the prosecutors never found out why they had committed the burglary. Sirica ordered a new grand jury to probe the causes of Watergate and related crimes.

There was no way that Watergate could be hidden now. No one realized that more than John Wesley Dean III.

"Two of the Finest . . ."

Someone would have to take the blame for the Watergate disaster. Dean felt he was being set up to take the fall. Nixon asked him to write a full report on Watergate. If he did, he would have to mention his own role. He stalled, knowing that such a report might be used against him.[12]

Dean contacted a lawyer. During the day, he pretended to work on the report. At night, he spilled his secrets to government prosecutors. Dean was bargaining for immunity from prosecution, which meant he could not be punished for statements admitting his illegal deeds. He was not alone. Jeb Magruder was also talking to authorities and cutting a deal. Both described their roles, plus those of Haldeman, Ehrlichman, and Mitchell.

Prosecutors took the stories to Assistant Attorney General Henry Petersen, and Petersen went to Attorney General Kleindienst. Both went to Nixon on April 15.

Haldeman and Ehrlichman must be fired, they told him. Nixon said he would think about it.

Later that day Nixon met with Dean. The counsel recalled it as a strange meeting. Nixon, he said, kept asking him pointed questions. It seemed as if he were tape-recording the conversation. At one point, Nixon moved over to a corner. In a low voice, he said he was only kidding about offering hush money to the burglars.

The next day Nixon gave Dean two letters. One was for the counsel's resignation, and the other was for a leave of absence. Both letters had Dean accepting the blame for the Watergate break-in. Dean refused to sign either letter. He would not resign unless Haldeman and Ehrlichman did likewise.

Ehrlichman, meanwhile, convinced the president that Mitchell's case was hopeless. Too many people claimed he approved plans for the break-in. Mitchell refused to accept any blame. "I considered John Mitchell to be one of my few close friends," Nixon wrote.[13] Yet he was willing to sell Mitchell down the river.

In early April, Nixon was indecisive. He had to get rid of renegade Dean. He did not want to lose Haldeman and Ehrlichman, but he knew crimes could be traced to them.

On April 18 Petersen and Kleindienst got more disturbing news. Grand jury testimony by Fred LaRue linked Hunt and Liddy to the break-in at psychiatrist Lewis Fielding's office for the Daniel Ellsberg files. Petersen thought it was shocking. He found it strange that Nixon did not appear surprised by the news.[14] Petersen and Kleindienst told Nixon they would inform Matthew Byrne, judge of the Ellsberg trial.

During this time, L. Patrick Gray was floundering in the United States Senate. He had kept demanding to be named permanent FBI director. Finally, Nixon nominated him for the post. The Senate had to confirm the nomination.

The Senate Judiciary Committee interviewed Gray. It turned out to be a disaster. Gray admitted to letting Dean sit in on FBI interviews with suspects of Watergate-related crimes. When someone asked him what happened to the documents Dean had given him, he said he had burned them during the Christmas holiday. A candidate for law enforcement director destroying evidence? His confirmation was doomed.

He received no help from the White House. The humiliated Gray withdrew his request to be permanent director, then resigned from the temporary position in late April.

The president spoke to the nation on April 30, 1973. "There is no whitewash in the White House," he proclaimed.[15] Even though he did not know the facts about Watergate until March, he would have a thorough investigation. Nixon said he had accepted the resignations of H. R. Haldeman and John Ehrlichman, "two of the finest public servants it has been my privilege to know."[16] Nixon also said that Dean had resigned, although Dean had given no such notice.

Nixon's speech left more questions than it answered. Why did Nixon, a man known for his intelligence, not know facts about the break-in until nine months after it occurred? If Haldeman and Ehrlichman were such great public servants, why were they leaving?

AMERICA'S POLITICAL SOAP OPERA

Let others wallow in Watergate," said Nixon in the summer of 1973.[1] By that time, many Americans were wallowing. Millions watched in fascination as a parade of witnesses provided details about an unusual collection of crimes.

A Simple Country Lawyer

Shortly after the 1972 election, Senate Majority Leader Mike Mansfield proposed a special committee to examine election irregularities. The United States Senate voted 70–0 on February 7 to establish the special committee. It was given the power to investigate irregularities in the 1972 presidential campaign. Officially its title was the Senate Select Committee on Presidential Campaign Activities. Most people called it the Senate Watergate Committee.

Four Democrats and three Republicans made up the committee. None had been a presidential candidate, and none was nationally known. The lack of fame was intentional. Members wanted to draw attention to witnesses' testimony, not themselves.

Samuel Ervin, an aging North Carolina Democrat, chaired the committee. Ervin was not, as he liked to claim, a simple country lawyer. He freely quoted Shakespeare and the Bible. Senators from both parties admired his knowledge of the Constitution.

Senator Howard Baker of Tennessee was the ranking Republican committee member. He tried to be impartial, yet also tried not to harm fellow Republican Nixon. Florida Republican Edward Gurney was openly pro-Nixon. Lowell Weicker, a Connecticut Republican, was less interested in protecting the president. Using members of his staff, he conducted his own separate investigation.

Georgia's Herman Talmadge, Hawaii's Daniel Inouye, and New Mexico's Joseph Montoya were the other three Democrats. None of the three stated an opinion about Watergate beforehand. All would be shocked by what they heard.

Executive Privilege

From the beginning there were disagreements, and from the beginning Ervin took charge. Republicans wanted shortened hearings, starting with the major witnesses. Ervin wanted lesser-ranked witnesses to testify first. They could set the foundation for questions to higher-ranked persons.

Newly appointed Special Prosecutor Archibald Cox wanted to postpone the hearings. If guilty parties testified in the Watergate hearings, it might be more difficult to convict them in court. Ervin replied that it was:

> more important for the committee to inform Congress and the American people what high officials entrusted by the President with enormous governmental and political power had done than it was for the courts to send a few people to jail.[2]

Nixon tried to use the power of executive privilege to limit the committee's findings. The president was the head of the nation's executive branch, and the executive branch was equal to Congress, the legislative branch. Under executive privilege, Nixon claimed Congress could not make demands of the president or his staff. The president did not have to answer a congressional summons.

He offered a compromise. Staff members would testify, but not under oath or in person. Ervin snapped, "That is not executive privilege. That is executive poppycock."[3] Nixon finally permitted his staff to testify, although he refused to do so himself.

At first television networks rotated their coverage of the hearings. That way soap opera fans would not miss their favorite shows. Soon Americans forgot other programs. This real-life political soap opera was the most popular show of all.

Reporters and television cameras did not change the solemn mood of the hearings. Ervin set the tone in his opening statement. If the charges against the Watergate burglars were true, Ervin said, then the burglars were trying to steal "not the jewels, money, or other property of American citizens, but something more valuable—their most precious heritage, the right to vote in a free election."[4]

Early Witnesses

More than three hundred spectators, including Daniel Ellsberg, crowded into the Senate caucus room on May 17, 1973. They heard leadoff witness Robert Odle say that he showed G. Gordon Liddy how to operate a shredding machine on the afternoon following the break-in.

The next day James McCord testified. Judge Sirica had told him that the length of his jail sentence would depend on how well he cooperated with the Watergate Committee. McCord more than happily talked. He claimed that John Mitchell, John Dean, and Jeb Magruder all approved the Watergate break-in early in 1972. He told how Jack Caulfield contacted him in January, offering clemency if

McCord pleaded guilty and did not cooperate with prosecutors. He also said Caulfield had added that if McCord refused to plead guilty, the administration would "have to take steps to defend itself."[5]

Former CRP Treasurer Hugh Sloan also testified. He told of massive quantities of money that passed from the CRP to unknown destinations. He said he had resigned from the CRP rather than lie in court about the amount of money being handled. An admiring Ervin said of Sloan, "an honest man is the noblest work of God."[6]

Jeb Magruder had not always been an honest man. He admitted to the Senate Committee that he had committed perjury at the Watergate trial. He also told many other things. Magruder said the Watergate break-in was only one of many White House wrongdoings. He described the activities of Haldeman, Ehrlichman, Dean, Mitchell, Colson, and several others. However, he stopped short of implicating President Richard M. Nixon. John W. Dean would handle that task.

Enemies

Ordinarily, summit conferences push all other news to the side. Journalists and the public wait anxiously for the results of talks between leaders of the most powerful nations. These decisions, after all, could affect the entire world.

Leonid Brezhnev, premier of the Soviet Union, visited the United States in 1973. The conference delayed the Watergate hearings for a week. Many Americans objected. To them, the words of a world leader were less interesting than those of a former White House lawyer.

John Dean's lawyers had bargained with the Watergate Committee for weeks. He received limited immunity.

Dean testified for a week. His opening statement alone was 245 pages long.

Dean focused on four conversations he had with Nixon. He told the senators how Nixon congratulated him last September 15 for stopping the investigation. He mentioned a March 13 conversation regarding hush money for the burglars. He talked about the "cancer on the presidency" conversation with Nixon on March 21. Dean also described the April 15 discussion. That was the day Nixon appeared to ask leading questions, then whispered something from the corner of the room.

Dean also revealed a shocking secret. The White House had kept a list of people and organizations considered hostile to Nixon's administration. More than two hundred names appeared on this "enemies list."

It covered business executives, labor leaders, most major Democrats, newspaper publishers and columnists, and even entertainers. Liberal Senator Edward Kennedy landed on the list. So did conservative former Alabama Governor George Wallace. Paul Newman, an actor who usually supported Democrats, made the enemies list. So did Joe Namath, a football player of no known political convictions. The "enemies" had nothing in common except that for some reason they displeased Richard Nixon. Dean said the White House never followed through on plans to take action against them.

Dean's charges, if true, could lead to impeachment. Richard Nixon could be forced from office. Yet there was no proof. Dean seemed to possess an amazing memory. He was calm and composed. Still, it was only the word of an unhappy former employee against the president of the United States. Many, if not most, Americans needed more proof than that.

Tales of the Tapes

Those who wanted confirmation of Dean's testimony would not get it from former Campaign Director John Mitchell. Time and time again he denied approving the Gemstone plan that included the break-in. He said that when he heard of the break-in, he did not tell Nixon. At that time, to Mitchell, Nixon's re-election was more important than anything else. He did not want to disturb his friend and boss with bad news before the election.

Former Haldeman aide Alexander Butterfield testified on July 16. His testimony would be, perhaps, the most important in the hearings. Butterfield told the senators that Nixon's White House conversations had been tape recorded since 1971.

Stunned silence greeted Butterfield's testimony. Then someone simply said, "Wow!"[7] Now there was a way to determine the truth. The tapes could show that Richard Nixon was telling the truth and John Dean was lying. Of course, they could also tell a completely different story.

It was a story Richard Nixon apparently did not want told. He refused to hand over the tapes after the Senate Committee subpoenaed them. Nixon's new chief of staff, Alexander Haig, immediately shut down the taping system. He and other advisors debated whether to destroy the tapes.

Nixon decided to keep them. After all, Presidents Kennedy and Johnson had recorded others' conversations without their knowledge. Nixon considered the tapes his private property. No one could force him to yield them.

"What a Liar!"

After Butterfield, Nixon's two former top advisors spoke. John Ehrlichman snarled at the questioning senators.

He said Dean had lied about Ehrlichman telling him to "deep six" the documents. He never promised Colson that executive clemency would be offered to E. Howard Hunt. By the time he had finished, Ehrlichman had contradicted the testimony of eighteen previous witnesses. Senator Daniel Inouye could take no more. He leaned back in his chair and muttered, "What a liar!"[8] His microphone was on, and viewers all over the country heard his opinion.

The often-surly Haldeman spoke in the opposite tone. The one-time tiger of Nixon's staff turned into a pussycat. He quietly, meekly, and politely evaded the senators' questions. He could not recall when he first heard about Watergate. He could not remember aide Gordon Strachan's warning of a Liddy bugging scheme. He had no idea how three hundred thousand dollars could have been removed from a cash fund he controlled.

He did remember Nixon's tapes. In fact, he said that the tapes proved his former boss innocent. How did he know? He had borrowed two key tapes and listened to them at home.

Ervin erupted when he heard this statement. "The United States Senate can't hear these tapes and you, a private citizen, can?" he asked.[9] Haldeman's statement only steeled the senators' determination to hear what evidence the tapes could give.

The Watergate Committee was adjourned from early August until late September. By that time, public interest in the committee testimony had waned.

August 1973 was not a dead time, however. A new, entirely different scandal was on the horizon.

6 Chapter

"I WILL NOT RESIGN IF INDICTED!"

Richard M. Nixon's popularity had skidded throughout the Senate Watergate hearings. Even so, few Americans want-ed to see him removed from office. Some did not believe there was enough evidence to remove him. Others felt the Watergate investigation was an attack by bitter Democrats upset at having lost the last election. Others feared the vice president. If Nixon were gone, Spiro T. Agnew would become president.

Spiro Who?

Spiro Agnew's rise in politics was not swift; it was mete-oric. In 1962 the forty-four-year-old Agnew was executive of Maryland's Baltimore County. Four years later he became the state's governor. In 1968, Richard Nixon chose him as vice-presidential running mate. From political unknown less than seven years earlier, Agnew could become the second-highest ranking official in the United States.

Republicans and Democrats alike were surprised about this unfamiliar candidate. "Spiro who?" many people asked.[1] Why did Nixon choose Agnew, when many other, better-known Republicans were available?

Nixon had his reasons. Agnew came from Maryland, a state the Republicans had a chance of winning. He had a reputation as a moderate or liberal governor, in contrast to the conservative Nixon image. Perhaps most important, Nixon sought a little-known running mate who would not distract attention from himself.

From the beginning, Agnew appeared to be a disaster. His thoughtless comments upset many ethnic groups. In one speech he said, "If you've seen one slum, you've seen them all."[2] To some, that remark showed he did not care about poor people. At one rally, a heckler raised a banner that read, "Apologize now, Spiro, it will save time later."[3]

When Nixon became president, Agnew went on the attack. He criticized antiwar demonstrators, intellectuals, and anyone else who opposed the Nixon administration. These attacks made him a favorite target of Nixon enemies. At the same time, the attacks gained him support among middle-aged, middle-class Americans who Nixon called the "silent majority."

Few Nixon administration officials avoided involvement in the Watergate scandals. Agnew was one and Henry Kissinger was another. Nixon consulted with foreign affairs advisor Kissinger almost daily about China, the Soviet Union, and the Middle East. He all but ignored his vice president. "The Nixon-Agnew relationship was virtually nonexistent," noted conservative commentator Howard Phillips.[4] Agnew stayed free of the Watergate intrigue. As it turned out, he had a scandal of his own.

Nolo Contendere

Stories began circulating in the summer of 1973 that Agnew had been accepting bribes for years. Workers under him had been forced to kick back, or give him, part of their salaries when he served in Maryland. Justice Department officials told Nixon of the Agnew crimes in June. Attorney General Elliot Richardson said he had never seen a stronger case against anyone. Agnew could be indicted on forty or more counts, or specific charges.

The *Wall Street Journal* ran the story on August 7. It claimed Agnew was guilty of extortion, bribery, and tax evasion. He had been taking bribes even while serving as vice president. Agnew went to Nixon for help. Nixon, however, had his own problems. He was not about to help a dead duck vice president.

By mid-September, Agnew appeared doomed. He wanted another meeting with President Nixon. Chief of Staff Alexander Haig told him that if he were indicted, Nixon would call for his resignation.

Agnew decided to try and cut a deal. He would plead guilty to a single tax evasion charge, but no felony charges. The Justice Department was ready to proceed with the case. Prosecutors had a certain victory. "We've got the evidence. We've got it cold," Assistant Attorney General Henry Petersen claimed.[5]

These remarks infuriated the vice president. He then tried to take his case to the public. He proclaimed his innocence before the National Federation of Republican Women. "I will not resign if indicted!" he shouted. "I will not resign if indicted!"[6]

Before long, though, reality set in. He was obviously guilty. If he went to trial, he could face prison time. If found guilty, he would lose the hefty vice- presidential pension he had earned.

On October 10 Agnew gave in. He pleaded *nolo contendere* in a Baltimore court. The plea meant he would not contest the court's decision. Agnew was fined $10,000 and placed on probation for one to three years. As part of the agreement, he resigned as vice president.

It was a humiliating experience for Spiro Agnew. In court, he was forced to listen as the Justice Department read seventy pages of charges against him. When Judge Matthew Hoffman asked Agnew if, by his plea, he admitted that the Justice Department "is possessed of sufficient evidence to prove its case beyond a reasonable doubt," Agnew responded, "I do."[7]

The day before Agnew's resignation, Nixon wished his running mate the best of luck. They never spoke again.

"Can You See Gerald Ford . . . ?"

The Agnew resignation meant a possible crisis. Carl Albert, speaker of the House of Representatives, was next in line to become president. Albert did not want the job. Even his fellow Democrats did not want him to assume the presidency. Republicans, after all, had won the 1972 election. If Richard Nixon were removed from office, his successor should also be a Republican.

After John F. Kennedy's assassination in 1963, the United States had been without a vice president. Soon afterward, the Twenty-fifth Amendment was added to the Constitution. The president would nominate a vice president, and this choice would be confirmed by a majority of both houses of Congress.

John Connally was Nixon's first choice for vice president. The former Texas governor had once been Nixon's secretary of the treasury. He remained an informal advisor. Still, Democrats had majorities in both the Senate and House of Representatives. They were not about to approve Democrat-turned-Republican Connally.

Nixon needed someone who could be confirmed. That someone turned out to be Gerald Ford, minority leader of the House of Representatives. Members of both parties liked the genial Ford, but few talked of his intellectual abilities. Nixon once scornfully commented to New York Governor Nelson Rockefeller, "Can you see Gerald Ford sitting in this [Oval Office presidential] chair?"[8]

Richard Nixon might have thought that Gerald Ford was impeachment insurance. He hoped Congress members, knowing Ford's limitations, would be too afraid of the possibility of Ford becoming president to remove Nixon from office.[9]

Congress, however, confirmed Ford. If something happened to Nixon, Gerald Ford would become president.

Chapter 7

"SATURDAY NIGHT MASSACRE"

Richard Nixon wasted little time mourning Agnew's fall. He had other business on his mind. "Now that we have disposed of [the Agnew] matter," he told Attorney General Elliot Richardson, "we can get rid of Cox."[1]

Nixon referred to Archibald Cox, special prosecutor for Watergate and related crimes. The president would soon remove this unwanted investigator, but it would come at a terrible cost.

Special Prosecutor

Richard Nixon had no real need to dismiss Attorney General Richard Kleindienst when H. R. Haldeman, John Ehrlichman, and John Dean resigned at the end of April 1973. In fact, it was a disastrous move. Nixon wished to name Defense Secretary Elliot Richardson as the new attorney general. Richardson's appointment had to be approved by the Democrat-controlled Senate. They put a condition on the approval. Richardson must appoint an independent special prosecutor. This officer's sole job would be to prosecute Watergate-related crimes. When Richardson agreed, the Senate confirmed him.

Richardson found such an officer. Archibald Cox was not someone Nixon would have chosen. Cox had served in the Justice Department under Presidents Kennedy and Johnson. Henry Kissinger commented that Cox had been "frantically anti-Nixon all the time I'd known him."[2] Even Cox was surprised by the appointment. He questioned Richardson how he got Nixon to agree to the appointment. "I never asked him," Richardson responded.[3]

Cox started his job assured of several powers. He could investigate other election-related frauds as well as the Watergate break-in. He could speak publicly whenever he wished and did not have to report to the attorney general. He had the power to grant immunity to witnesses. Only the attorney general could fire him and only for "extraordinary improprieties."[4]

The special prosecutor did not take long to show his independence. When the White House taping system became known in July, Cox immediately requested several tapes. Nixon cited executive privilege and refused to hand them over. Cox went to Judge John Sirica for a subpoena to receive the tapes. Nixon again refused to obey the subpoena. Cox even called out the twenty-three-member grand jury that looked into Watergate crimes. Every grand juror requested the tapes. Nixon would not budge.

Tapes Delay

Spring and summer of 1973 were not kind to Richard Nixon. In May, Judge Matthew Byrne threw out the case against Daniel Ellsberg. He pointed to the break-in of Dr. Fielding's office. He also revealed that Ehrlichman had approached him during the trial with an offer to become FBI director. Byrne cited these moves as examples of government interference in the case. A grand jury indicted Ehrlichman, Young, and others for the Fielding break-in.

There were other mounting problems. Several large corporations admitted to making illegal contributions to the Committee to Re-Elect the President. Owners claimed the White House pressured them to make the contributions. The General Services Administration (GSA) told that $17 million in government money had gone to refurbish private Nixon homes in San Clemente, California, and Key Biscayne, Florida. A memo addressed to the Senate Watergate Committee disclosed that a company called International Telephone and Telegraph (ITT) had made payments to the Republican Committee. In return for the money, the Justice Department offered to drop a lawsuit against the giant communications company.

The tapes remained Nixon's most important problem. At first he claimed he needed to protect the confidentiality of his conversations. Then he claimed the nation's security was at stake. Later he said the tapes would prove him innocent of any wrongdoing.

Critics did not believe these explanations. The need to uncover criminal activity was more important than a right to a private conversation. Nixon gave no proof of a threat to national security.

"There must be real dirt on the tapes. Otherwise he wouldn't be fighting so hard," Kissinger commented. Someone asked him if Nixon might be worried about preserving the powers of the presidency. "He cares about the office," Kissinger said, "but he cares about Richard Nixon more."[5]

Judge Sirica did not accept Nixon's argument that the tapes proved his innocence. "If Nixon himself were not involved, why would he stand on such an abstract principle as executive privilege when by voluntarily turning over the tapes he could prove himself innocent?" he commented later.[6] On August 29, Sirica ordered Nixon to turn over the tapes for Sirica's private inspection. Nixon immediately appealed the judge's decision. The United States Court of Appeals upheld Sirica.

Nixon would have to turn over something. He hoped it would not be the tapes themselves, which could be used as evidence in court. They could prove his guilt and that of his staff members. Instead, he sought a compromise. He would turn over written transcripts of the requested tapes. A neutral third party could listen to the tapes and verify them against the manuscripts.

Mississippi Senator John Stennis was Nixon's choice to be that third party. Other senators acknowledged Stennis's honesty. Still, Stennis was a Nixon ally who could be persuaded that the Watergate operation might be justified under national security. He also had poor hearing. Most important, a transcript verified by him could not be admitted as evidence. "[Nixon's] proposal was absolutely unacceptable to me," Cox said.[7]

Nixon aide Alexander Haig told Cox that the Stennis proposal was Nixon's final offer. Furthermore, the president would turn over no new materials to the grand jury, and Cox could not subpoena any new materials.

Triumph and Disaster

The religious holiday of Yom Kippur should have been a day of quiet reflection for Israel's Jews. Instead, October 6, 1973, was a day of war. Egyptians from the southwest and Syrians from the north invaded Israeli territory. Some people feared that hostile Arab neighbors would overrun Israel. Others worried that this conflict might lead to a world war between the United States and the Soviet Union.

Nixon and Kissinger helped control the crisis. The United States airlifted supplies to Israel. Those goods helped Israel's army drive the Arab states back to the previous borders in a matter of days. Meanwhile, Kissinger flew to Moscow and convinced the Soviets to stay out of the battle. It was the Nixon administration's finest hour.

Considerably worse hours were passing at home, however. By mid-October, Richard Nixon was determined that Archibald Cox must go. Dismissing him was Elliot Richardson's job.

Haig called Richardson and told him that the president wanted Cox fired. Richardson refused such an order from anyone except Nixon himself. He told Haig that Cox had done nothing improper. He resigned rather than fire Cox.

Next, Haig tried William Ruckelshaus. The deputy attorney general would not fire the special prosecutor either. Nixon fired Ruckelshaus before he could submit a resignation. The third person in line, Solicitor General Robert Bork, finally agreed to discharge Cox.

These dismissals took place on Saturday, October 20. That night Press Secretary Ron Ziegler announced the Richardson resignation and the firings. He added that the president had abolished the office of special prosecutor. Meanwhile, Haig ordered the FBI to seal off the offices of Cox, Richardson, and Ruckelshaus.

The action stunned the nation. It became known as the "Saturday Night Massacre." Some feared for the safety of the government. If the president took such actions to stop an investigation against him, what would prevent him from attacking the Congress and courts? "A government of laws may be on the verge of becoming the government of one man," Richardson commented.[8]

Illinois Republican Congressman John Anderson had a more accurate prediction. He said, "Impeachment resolutions are going to be raining down like hailstones."[9]

8 Chapter

"SINISTER FORCES"

According to the U.S. Constitution, even the president can be removed from office. Article II, Section 4 says the president "shall be removed from office on impeachment for, and conviction of, treason, bribery, or other high crimes and misdemeanors."

The House of Representatives is able to impeach a president. This means the representatives believe there is enough evidence to remove him. If a majority of representatives vote against him, the president is impeached. Then the case goes to the Senate. A special committee presents evidence against the president. If two thirds of the senators vote for conviction, the president is out of office.

Some Congresspersons cringed at the word *impeachment*. They knew about the case of Andrew Johnson, a Democrat who became president after the Civil War. Johnson took over when Republican Abraham Lincoln was assassinated. The House impeached Johnson. He escaped Senate removal by one vote. Historians generally believe Johnson was tried unfairly. Republicans wanted to oust him for purely political reasons. Congress members might have been willing to impeach Richard Nixon. Yet they would demand proof of his misdeeds.

Congress met the Tuesday following the Saturday Night Massacre. Immediately, twenty-one representatives offered resolutions of impeachment. Debate went on for forty-five minutes before anyone spoke in Nixon's favor. Republicans were sending Nixon a message. If he did not turn over the tapes, they would desert him.

Missing Tapes and Gaps

Nixon miscalculated when he ordered Cox fired. He did not realize public reaction against him would be so fierce. In 1972 *Time* named Richard Nixon and Henry Kissinger "Men of the Year." In late 1973 the news magazine printed the first editorial in its fifty years, calling for Nixon's resignation. "Richard Nixon and the nation have passed a tragic point of no return," *Time* commented. "The nightmare certainly must be ended."[1]

Richard Nixon had no intention of resigning. However, he knew he had to make some compromises to keep his office. Nixon had hoped to abolish the special prosecutor and put the attorney general in charge of Watergate prosecution. That way, he could have more control over the investigation. He could prevent investigators from seeking his tapes.

Now, however, it was clear that like it or not, he would have to appoint another special prosecutor. Leon Jaworski, a highly respected Texas attorney, was his choice. This time, however, neither Nixon nor the attorney general could remove the special prosecutor. Removal required the agreement of Republican and Democratic leaders of the Senate and House, plus the leaders of the Senate and House judiciary committees.

Nixon knew that he would have to yield the tapes. They produced another problem. Two of the subpoenaed tapes did not exist. The June 20, 1972, telephone conversation with John Mitchell took place from the residential section of the White House. That part of the building lacked a recorder. The April 15 conversation with John Dean was not recorded either, because the machine had run out of tape.

But Nixon said he had notes of that meeting. He suggested to advisors J. Fred Buzhardt and Leonard Garment that he create a tape of the conversation and submit it to the grand jury. They were taken aback by the idea. How could the president, himself a lawyer, even think of creating false evidence?[2]

Another surprise awaited Judge Sirica. The key June 20, 1972, tape had several minutes of conversation missing. Former advisor H. R. Haldeman's notes verified that this "gap" covered a conversation about Watergate between Haldeman and Nixon.

Nixon's secretary Rose Mary Woods said she had erased part of the tape. She was transcribing the tape when the telephone rang. She said she reached back for the phone while accidentally pressing the "record" instead of the "stop" button and keeping her foot on a pedal. Woods claimed she held the position for about five minutes. The White House released a photograph of the secretary in the position she described. An acrobat, much less a secretary, could not have held that pose for five minutes. The loyal Woods did little with her testimony except humiliate herself. Besides, Woods said she erased only five minutes of tape. In all, eighteen and a half minutes were missing.

What caused the gap? Chief of Staff Alexander Haig hinted at "sinister forces."[3] Sirica believed the forces were human ones. A panel of recording experts appointed by the judge concluded that several different erasures had caused the gap.

Who erased the tapes? Haldeman guessed that Nixon himself might have done it. Whether he erased the tapes or not, Nixon recognized the consequences of the altered tape. "Most people think my inability to explain the eighteen and a half minute gap is the most unbelievable and insulting part of the whole of Watergate," he commented in his memoirs.[4]

Nixon's crises mounted in November. A newspaper reported that he earned more than $200,000 in 1970 but paid only $793 in taxes. He made a similar amount of money in 1972 but paid only $4,300. The president discussed his finances in a television address on November 17. "I've never profited from public service," he claimed. "People have the right to know whether their President is a crook. Well, I am not a crook."[5]

Crooked or not, many of Nixon's tax deductions were against the law. In April 1974 the Joint Congressional Committee on Taxation reviewed Nixon's tax records. The committee ruled that several of his deductions, including those for his vice-presidential papers, were illegal. Nixon agreed to pay $476,431 in back taxes.

Operation Candor

Richard Nixon still had allies. His family, especially his daughter Julie, openly backed him. Friends Bebe Rebozo and Robert Abplanalp remained loyal. A Providence, Rhode Island, rabbi named Baruch Korff took out a full-page ad in *The New York Times* defending the president. Alexander Haig and Press Secretary Ron Ziegler were constant advisors.

Nixon also had some allies in Congress, though not many. In late 1973 he invited Republicans and Southern Democrats to discuss Watergate with him. Nixon called these discussions Operation Candor.

The operation was not entirely successful. Some Republicans and even a few Democrats remained solidly behind him, but many Republicans resented that Nixon had done little to help their campaigns in 1972. They owed him nothing. Some were not willing to support Nixon unless he turned over the requested tapes. Several Republicans secretly hoped Nixon would resign. They feared the Nixon scandals might mean a disaster for their party in the 1974 elections.

Richard Nixon addressed Congress in late January 1974. During the annual State of the Union Address, he declared, "One year of Watergate is enough!"[6] Booing Democrats obviously did not agree.

Those boos meant little. Nixon would have liked their support, but he did not need it to stay in office. If all Democrats voted against him, he would be impeached. However, he could survive if fewer than two thirds of the senators voted to convict. He felt confident that he had the thirty-four Senate votes needed. Besides, most Americans polled still opposed impeachment. They wanted the "smoking pistol," evidence that proved beyond any doubt that Richard Nixon was guilty. The representatives would surely watch the poll results.

"What Did the President Know . . . ?"

The beginning of 1974 was no better for Richard Nixon than the end of 1973. His legal counsel, Charles Alan Wright, resigned in January. Wright was angry at not being allowed to listen to the tapes. Nixon named a Boston attorney, James St. Clair, to lead his legal team.

Nixon's poll ratings collapsed every month. As late as April 15, 1973, he had enjoyed a 60 percent favorable rating in the Gallup Poll. That rating tumbled to 31 percent in August, during the Senate Watergate hearings. By late January it was 23 percent, an all-time low for a president.

Demands kept pouring in for the tapes and other evidence. New Special Prosecutor Jaworski sought more than twenty tapes in early January. When Nixon refused, Jaworski warned that not turning over the tapes might be an impeachable offense. Jaworski requested sixty-four additional tapes on April 16. Judge Sirica issued a subpoena two days later.

The Senate Watergate Committee concluded its testimony in late 1973. Now it wanted nearly five hundred documents. Nixon said no. Once again, the president claimed that turning over the material would destroy the confidentiality of his conversations. Senator Howard Baker's frequently asked question—what did the president know, and when did he know it?—would remain unanswered for now.

When the Watergate grand jury asked Nixon to testify, lawyer St. Clair sought a compromise. Would the grand jury accept answers in writing? No, it would not, the jury responded. In that case, the president declined to appear.

Former advisor John Ehrlichman also sought Nixon's testimony. He claimed that he was following Nixon's orders when he arranged the break-in of Daniel Ellsberg's psychiatrist's office. Nixon's attorneys advised that Nixon "respectfully decline to appear."[7]

The House Judiciary Committee also sought information. Committee members voted to grant Chairman Peter Rodino subpoena power. The House of Representatives later gave Rodino the power by a 410–4 vote. Rodino immediately subpoenaed tapes and other documents.

"Unindicted Co-conspirator"

On March 1, the Watergate grand jury handed down indictments against seven former Nixon administration officials. Former Chief of Staff H. R. Haldeman, former Domestic Affairs Advisor John Ehrlichman, former United States Attorney General and CRP Director John Mitchell, former Special Counsel Charles Colson, former Haldeman aide Gordon Strachan, former Assistant Attorney General Robert Mardian, and CRP attorney Kenneth Parkinson all faced criminal charges. These charges included conspiracy with other persons "known and unknown" to obstruct justice, to arrange hush money for Watergate burglars, to offer executive clemency, and to destroy documents.[8] "There had never been such wholesale criminal proceedings against the top men in the administration of an American president," Sirica noted.[9]

Nixon avoided indictment. His lawyers questioned whether he, as president, could be indicted. Any trial of political figures would be difficult enough without including this constitutional issue.

However, Watergate prosecutors did not want to pretend that Nixon might not have been involved in illegal activities. They also wanted to assure that evidence of his taped conversations could be used in criminal trials on the case. Richard Nixon was named an "unindicted co-conspirator."[10] He was not charged with any crime, but was considered to be involved in Watergate-related activities. The grand jury, however, did not announce Nixon's status.

"Expletive Deleted"

Both Judge Sirica and Judiciary Chairman Rodino stepped up their demands for Nixon's tapes. The tapes put Nixon in a dilemma. If he held onto them, impeachment was almost certain. Release them (particularly the June 23 tape) and conviction was likely. Nixon sought another alternative.

Nixon hastily edited manuscripts of the tapes. He removed material that he considered irrelevant, including words he considered obscene. He would release these materials instead of the requested tapes.

Haig met with Jaworski on April 28. He showed the special prosecutor a fifty-page statement Nixon planned to issue the following evening. Jaworski was not satisfied with this proposal.

Nevertheless, Nixon went on television on April 29. Behind him were blue bound books that looked like a set of encyclopedias. The 1,308-page document was titled *Submission of Recorded Presidential Conversations to the Committee of the Judiciary of the House of Representatives by Richard Nixon*. The president said the material "will tell it all."[11]

It told a lot. Americans did not like what they heard or read. Pages were peppered with foul words, noted as "expletive deleted." The transcripts showed Richard Nixon as a rude, mean man who had little or no regard for other people. He referred to former FBI Director L. Patrick Gray as "that dumb dumb Gray." Supreme Court Justice William Rehnquist was part of "that group of clowns we have around here." Jeb Stuart Magruder, who lied in court to defend the president, was called "a rather weak man . . . sort of a light weight in a very heavy job."[12]

Parts of key conversations disappeared. They were replaced by "inaudible" or "unintelligible." Observers noted that the recording device worked perfectly for trivial conversations. Yet, as Professor William B. Todd observed, there were 367 "inaudible" remarks in one short conversation.[13]

Nixon's compromise attempt failed. Two days after his address, the House Judiciary Committee ruled that he had failed to comply with its subpoena. Once again, the president cited executive privilege. He refused to hand over the actual tapes.

The *Chicago Tribune* supported Nixon for president three times. It had a reputation as a "Republican" newspaper. Even the *Tribune* had had enough. The paper called for Nixon's impeachment. An editorial commented, "We have seen the private man and we are appalled."[14]

"Are You Running for Something?"

Richard Nixon's other defenses were not working. Prosecutors and the House Judiciary Committee did not accept executive privilege. Neither the courts nor Congress considered Nixon's manuscripts adequate. Richard Nixon would take his case to the American people. He would show he was a useful and necessary president.

Nixon went anywhere and everywhere to raise himself in public opinion. He once showed up at Nashville, Tennessee's Grand Ole Opry Park. Surprised Oprygoers watched their chief executive crack jokes, play the piano, and swing a yo-yo.

He addressed the National Association of Broadcasters in Houston. Reporter Dan Rather tried to get his attention. Then Nixon asked Rather, "Are you running for something?" Rather replied, "No, sir, Mr. President, are you?"[15]

Gerald Ford gave up his seat in Congress when he became vice president. Voters in his Michigan district chose his successor in April. Nixon traveled throughout the district. Despite (or perhaps because of) Nixon's campaigning, the Republican candidate lost the seat.

French President Georges Pompidou died in April 1974. Nixon attended the Paris funeral. Without giving notice, he left his limousine to shake people's hands, as if he were a politician running for office.

Nixon considered the Middle East the site of a diplomatic triumph. He went there in early June. Throngs of cheering Egyptians greeted him along the parade route.

Yet Nixon's popularity among the French and Egyptians meant nothing. In mid-1974 thirty-eight people would decide his fate—the members of the House Judiciary Committee.

"THE SMOKING PISTOL"

After the impeachment resolutions had been introduced in October, the House Judiciary Committee began its work. The committee spent nearly half a year gathering evidence from any sources available. The Senate Watergate Committee provided some testimony. Civil lawsuits and grand jury testimony provided other information. Judge Sirica turned over a briefcase full of documents. The committee demanded any and all evidence. It accepted no excuses.

The staff investigated the Watergate break-in and cover-up, plus evidence from other areas. These included illegal use of government agencies for political purposes, "dirty tricks," Nixon's finances, and the secret bombing of Cambodia. It also considered whether to impeach Nixon for impounding funds, or refusing to spend money appropriated by Congress.

On May 9, 1974, Committee Counsel John Doar was ready to present the evidence. Rodino pounded his gavel. Impeachment proceedings were underway.

A Cross Section

Carl Albert, as speaker of the House, had determined which committee would handle impeachment matters. He chose the Judiciary Committee, chaired by Peter Rodino. Judiciary had handled the vice-presidential confirmation of Gerald Ford. Albert thought Rodino had done a good job. Rodino was no household name, but he had a reputation for being fair and impartial.

Rodino's committee was a cross section of America. John Conyers and Charles Rangel represented inner-city neighborhoods of Detroit and New York City. William Cohen served coastal areas of Maine. Californian Charles Wiggins represented Whittier, Richard Nixon's old district. Hamilton Fish, from affluent upstate New York, also served on the committee.

The committee also contained people with a variety of demeanors. Calm, polite Rodino contrasted with sharp-tongued Texas Democrat Jack Brooks and New Jersey's Charles Sandman. Barbara Jordan, a Texan known for her political and verbal skills, served on the committee. So did Harold Donohue, a Massachusetts congressman who occasionally fell asleep during committee sessions.

The group also covered the political spectrum. Robert Kastenmeier of Madison, Wisconsin, was an outspoken liberal. Conyers and Rangel, along with other African Americans, appeared on the "enemies list." All appeared to be unquestionable votes for impeachment.

Nixon, however, had his allies. The committee's ranking Republican, Edward Hutchinson, said impeachment should only be charged on criminal grounds. Delbert Latta of Ohio and Trent Lott of Mississippi were both solid Nixon supporters.

The Judiciary Committee had twenty-one Democrats and seventeen Republicans. To avoid impeachment, the president would need two Democrats in his favor. Three Southern Democrats seemed most likely to provide these votes: Walter Flowers of Alabama, Ray Thornton of Arkansas, and James Mann of South Carolina. All represented districts won by Nixon in 1972.

However, Nixon would have to keep all seventeen Republicans on his side. There was no certainty he could do so. Maine's William Cohen, Robert McClory and Thomas Railsback both of Illinois, and Caldwell Butler of Virginia were moderate Republicans who could go either way. Butler and Cohen had already shown independence by seeking subpoenas of the presidential tapes.

The committee met in public for about twenty minutes, then went into closed session. Unlike the Senate Watergate Committee, the House Judiciary Committee hearings would not be open to the public. Two hundred million Americans, including Richard Milhous Nixon of 1600 Pennsylvania Avenue in Washington, D.C., would have to wait for the results.

"Deliberate . . . Deception"

While the Judiciary Committee heard testimony, other dramas took place. All of them meant bad news for Richard Nixon. On June 6 the *Los Angeles Times* disclosed Nixon's unindicted co-conspirator status. Many people still might not have known what an unindicted co-conspirator was. But they knew they did not want a president who was one.

The Senate Watergate Committee concluded its work on June 30. It released a final report a few days later. The report denounced the misuse of power by the president and his aides. It cited the Plumbers' break-in of Ellsberg's psychiatrist's office and abuse of the FBI, CIA, and Justice Department.

The Judiciary Committee made public nearly four thousand pages of evidence in early July. It also released its own transcripts of eight Nixon tapes. These accounts differed greatly from the transcripts Nixon had offered. In every case, the committee's version put the president in a worse light. The committee printed conversations omitted by the president. For example, on March 22, 1973, Nixon had told Mitchell, in reference to the Watergate burglars, "I want you all to stonewall it, let them plead the Fifth Amendment, cover up, or anything else."[1]

Doar presented his closing argument to the committee on July 19, 1974. He spoke about Nixon's "deliberate, contrived, continued, and continuing deception of the American people."[2] He claimed Nixon obstructed justice, abused the powers of the presidency, refused to honor subpoenas from the Judiciary Committee, and violated tax laws.

On July 23, Lawrence Hogan said he would vote for impeachment. This announcement worried Nixon. He expected defections from the liberals, but not from this conservative Maryland Republican. Now Nixon needed Democratic support more than ever. Nixon called George Wallace and asked him to influence Walter Flowers's vote. Wallace answered that he could not do so. Nixon turned to Haig. "Well, Al, there goes the presidency," he sighed.[3]

Disarming Decision

Battles still raged for control of Richard Nixon's tapes. Rodino and the Judiciary Committee still wanted the tapes they had subpoenaed from Nixon. He refused to produce them. Nixon held to his claim of executive privilege. He also said, without proof, that some tapes were so sensitive that he could not release them under any circumstances.

Rodino did not want to go to court over the tapes. The legislative branch of government, Rodino believed, was equal to the executive branch.[4] It should not need a court to have its orders obeyed. Besides, if Richard Nixon refused to hand over evidence, that lack of cooperation could be grounds for impeachment.

Special Prosecutor Leon Jaworski had no reservations about seeking the tapes. Nixon's arguments about separation of powers meant nothing to him. Both he and Nixon were from the executive branch of government.

Jaworski had tried negotiating with the Nixon team. If Nixon would turn over only eighteen tapes, Jaworski would forget about the rest. One of those tapes requested was the one from June 23. Nixon turned down all compromises.

With that refusal, Jaworski continued his pursuit. Nixon realized that Jaworski would mount a court challenge over the material. He hoped that the case would proceed through the Court of Appeals. If so, a decision before the Supreme Court might be delayed weeks or months.

Jaworski had no intention of waiting that long. On May 24 he appealed directly to the Supreme Court for a decision on the tapes case. A week later the Court agreed to hear the case.

Nixon had confidence in the Supreme Court. After all, he had appointed four of its members. Nixon appointee William Rehnquist, who had worked in Nixon's Justice Department, excused himself from the case. Yet Lewis Powell, Harry Blackmun, and Chief Justice Warren Burger were on the High Court because of Nixon. If the president could get a split opinion among the justices, he could argue that there was no consensus of opinion against him.

On July 24 the Court heard the case. Jaworski took an hour to make his opening argument. Nixon lawyer St. Clair had made the argument that the right to executive privilege was absolute. Therefore, the president did not have to answer subpoenas. Jaworski disagreed. "Shall the evidence from the White House be confined to what a single person, highly interested in the outcome, is willing to make available?" he asked.[5]

The Court's verdict was solid, and it devastated the president. All eight judges ruled that Nixon must turn over the subpoenaed tapes to Jaworski and the Watergate grand jury. "The unanimous decision had completely disarmed Nixon of whatever plans he had to disobey and circumvent the Court," Jaworski commented.[6]

Articles of Impeachment

That same day, the House Judiciary Committee began its impeachment debate. Five articles of impeachment would be discussed. "I as chairman have been guided by a simple principle, the principle that the law must deal fairly with every man," Rodino began.[7] Few argued that the chairman tried to be anything but fair. Republicans Butler, Cohen,

Railsback, and Fish were considered swing votes. So were Democrats Mann, Thornton, and Flowers. All seven moderates agreed that the evidence required impeachment. Rodino had them write the articles.

Americans sat gripped with suspense as the representatives helped decide the nation's fate. They heard serious heartfelt, and sometimes eloquent, comments from the thirty-eight men and women. Flowers noted that the Constitution's preamble read "We the People," not "We the public officials."[8] Railsback's emotional speech showed the unhappiness he felt in voting against a president who had helped him. Wiggins and Sandman angrily claimed that there was no specific evidence to prove Nixon's wrongdoing.

On July 27 committee members voted on Article I. This article claimed that Nixon had obstructed justice. It charged that Nixon "used the powers of his office both personally and through subordinates to cover up and conceal responsibility" for the Watergate break-in.[9] "I [had] the absolute feeling of sadness about the whole thing," Butler said.[10] He and five other Republicans joined all Democrats in voting for the article. This vote ensured that an impeachment resolution would go to the entire House.

The committee also voted on four other items. Article II charged that Nixon directed a "pattern of massive and persistent abuse of power for political purposes involving unlawful and unconstitutional invasion of the rights and privacy of individual citizens of the United States."[11] This article covered the wiretaps, the Ellsberg break-in, and attempts to block the FBI investigation of White House crimes. This resolution passed 28–10. The third article stated that Nixon "refused without cause to comply with the House for subpoenas issued by the House of Representatives."[12] It passed 21–17. Two other articles, dealing with Nixon's income taxes and the secret bombing of Cambodia, failed.

Debate in the full House of Representatives would begin in a few weeks. Preparations began even beyond the House. Republican and Democratic Senate leaders met on July 29 to discuss procedures for a trial. What ground rules were needed? Where should television cameras be placed? How should tickets be distributed? A year or even six months ago, such preparations seemed unthinkable. Now they appeared inevitable.

"My President Is a Liar!"

On the day of the Supreme Court decision, Nixon called J. Fred Buzhardt. "There might be a problem with the June 23 tape, Fred," the president told him.[13] A puzzled Buzhardt wondered what was wrong. Did the tape contain national security information? Were there additional gaps or erasures? It was worse, far worse. Buzhardt listened to the tape, then murmured, "It's over, it's all over now."[14]

Buzhardt had heard a conversation between H. R. Haldeman and Nixon. Haldeman explained the Watergate break-in to the president. He mentioned the laundered checks and said the problem originated with Mitchell. Haldeman suggested that the CIA persuade the FBI to drop its investigation. Then Nixon agreed with Haldeman's idea.

For months Richard Nixon had claimed that he knew nothing of Watergate before March 1973. This tape proved he knew about it six days after the break-in. Not only did he know about it, but he was planning to hide its details from the public. Buzhardt called Haig. "We've found the smoking pistol," he said.[15]

St. Clair heard the tape a few days later. As a lawyer, he knew what he must do. He could tell the Supreme Court what the June 23 tape contained, or he could persuade his client to change his plea. In Nixon's case that meant agreeing to resign.

Nixon could quit, or he could be fired. Impeachment was certain from the Democrat-controlled House. On July 31 former Republican Party Chairman Bob Dole told Nixon that fifty-eight to sixty senators appeared ready to convict Nixon.

More than honor lay at stake. If Nixon resigned before removal, he could receive an annual $60,000 pension plus $96,000 for staff salaries. If removed, he would lose that money.

On Thursday, August 1, Nixon told Haig he would resign. Haig then told Ford about Nixon's legal problems and offered various solutions. Nixon could stay in office. He could step aside until the impeachment issue was resolved. He could pardon himself, then resign. He could pardon himself and all Watergate defendants, then resign. He could agree to resign in exchange for a pardon from his successor. Ford and Haig discussed options but made no deals during this meeting.

The following day Nixon changed his mind. He was no quitter; he would fight his way out of the mess. Daughter Julie urged him to hang tough. So did his friend Bebe Rebozo.

His June 23 tape would be made public; this he knew. Yet maybe reaction would not be harsh. Maybe he could survive this crisis as he had survived so many others.

Several key Congress members received sealed envelopes on Monday, August 5. These included Republican leaders, Nixon defenders on the Judiciary Committee, and Democrats believed loyal to the president. The envelopes contained transcripts of the tape from June 23, 1972. A few hours later members of the press received the transcript.

The president went on television that night to minimize the damage. "I am firmly convinced that the record, in its entirety, does not justify the extreme step of impeachment and removal of a President," he said.[16]

He misjudged the nation. Nixon's already weak support evaporated. Wiggins, Nixon's strongest supporter on Judiciary, said, "The guys who stuck by the President were really led down the garden path, weren't we?"[17] He called for Nixon's resignation. Columnist James Kilpatrick, one of Nixon's strongest allies in the press, likewise was shocked. "We have been led astray. We have been lied to," Kilpatrick wrote. "My President is a liar!"[18]

Nixon called a Cabinet meeting for Tuesday, August 6. He tried to talk about the economy, but few Cabinet members listened to him. Even if he remained in office, he would be president in name only.

"I No Longer Have . . . a Political Base"

Arizona Senator Barry Goldwater dreaded this moment. For weeks he had avoided it. Now he had little choice. Goldwater paraded toward the White House with Senate Minority Leader Hugh Scott and House Minority Leader John Rhodes. The three veteran Republicans went to tell Richard Nixon he had no support in Congress. At most there were fifteen Senate votes, Scott estimated. Goldwater said only four votes were solid. For the good of the Republican party and the nation, Nixon must resign.

Nixon had other callers that day. His former top advisors, Haldeman and Ehrlichman, asked him to pardon them. Nixon refused to do so. His own legal future remained uncertain. He was not about to take a noose from their necks so that somebody might put one around his own.

That night Nixon met with Henry Kissinger. The president asked his advisor to pray with him. Kissinger told him that history would treat him more kindly than current journalists. Nixon replied, "It depends on who writes the history."[19]

By Thursday morning, August 8, Nixon still had not announced his plans. A huge headline in that afternoon's *Chicago Daily News* contained the single word: "When?"[20] By mid-afternoon, the world had its answer.

The president went on television at nine o'clock that evening. He delivered a speech that was short, and many believed, "graceless."[21] "It has become evident that I no longer have a strong enough political base in the Congress," he gave as his reason for stepping down.[22] He did not mention the actions he had taken which had caused Congress to oppose him.

Even critics had mixed emotions. The *Chicago Tribune* commented, "It is an occasion not for joy, but rather for gratitude, relief, and a renewal of hope."[23] Judge Sirica said of Richard Nixon, "I was sorry for him, but I was also relieved to see him go."[24]

". . . You Destroy Yourself"

A weary Richard Nixon spoke to his staff the following morning. One of his final remarks, in a way, summed up the entire Watergate crisis. "Always remember, others may hate you," President Richard Nixon said, "but those who hate you don't win unless you hate them, and then you destroy yourself."[25]

The Nixons and a few staff members boarded a helicopter that would take them to Air Force One. The presidential airplane would fly them to San Clemente, California. Just before entering the helicopter, Nixon raised both hands in a V-for-victory sign.

Just before noon, Secretary of State Henry Kissinger received a letter. It read, "I hereby resign the office of President of the United States." It contained Richard Nixon's signature. By this time the Nixon party's airplane was flying over the Midwest.

Minutes after noon, Richard Nixon ceased being president. His sixty-one-year-old vice president took his place. Gerald Ford uttered the words honored by most who came before him but nearly disgraced by his predecessor:

> I do solemnly swear that I will faithfully execute the Office of President of the United States, and will to the best of my Ability, preserve, protect and defend the Constitution of the United States.

10 Chapter

"OUR LONG NATIONAL NIGHTMARE"

For more than two years Watergate and its related scandals made the front pages of America's newspapers and the lead stories of the nightly news. For Americans, it was a fascinating drama and civics lesson.

Watergate changed the face of American politics. Some changes were good. Congress passed campaign reform legislation to prevent future election abuse. Media throughout the country kept a sharper eye on public officials. Yet one of the changes was unfortunate—a mistrust toward politics and politicians that continues to this day.

"Nixon Had Wrecked the Lives . . ."

Henry Kissinger noted, "In destroying himself, Nixon had wrecked the lives of almost all who had come into contact with him."[1] Forty-six individuals and thirteen corporations pleaded guilty, were indicted, or were convicted of Watergate-related charges.

The list of people serving prison time looked like a Who's Who of Nixon's early administration: H. R. Haldeman, John Ehrlichman, John Dean, John Mitchell, Charles

Colson, Jeb Stuart Magruder, Egil Krogh, Fred LaRue, Donald Segretti, Appointments Secretary Dwight Chapin, attorney Herb Kalmbach, Magruder assistant Bart Porter, G. Gordon Liddy, E. Howard Hunt, James McCord, Bernard Barker, Eugenio Martinez, Virgilio Gonzalez, and Frank Sturgis. Maurice Stans paid a $150,000 fine. David Young and Alfred Baldwin, in exchange for their testimony, escaped prison time. Richard Kleindienst received a one-month suspended sentence for not testifying fully to a congressional committee on the ITT matter.

Not everyone who experienced the Watergate affair was involved in the crimes. Some observers enjoyed notable careers afterward. Alexander Haig remained active in Republican politics. Patrick Buchanan, a Nixon speechwriter, became a conservative columnist and television commentator, and twice sought the Republican nomination for president. Bob Dole, the former Republican chairman, served more than thirty years in Congress. He was the Republican nominee for president in 1996.

Dan Rather, in 1974, asked Richard Nixon if he was running for office. Seven years later Rather became chief anchor of the *CBS Evening News.*

Few people outside of Washington, D.C., had heard of Bob Woodward or Carl Bernstein in June 1972. Two years later they were heroes to thousands of would-be investigative reporters. They helped the *Washington Post* win a Pulitzer Prize for journalism and co-wrote two best-selling books on Watergate.

Watergate brought out the best in some people. Sam Ervin and Peter Rodino were little known outside of Congress. Their roles on congressional committees won them respect throughout the nation. Previously obscure Judge John Sirica was named "Man of the Year" by *Time* in 1973.

Pardon

On Sunday, September 8, 1974, most Americans were relaxing. Those who were watching television or listening to the radio received a jolt. The White House press office announced that President Gerald Ford had pardoned Richard Nixon for all crimes he committed or might have committed in office.

There would be no Watergate trial for Richard Nixon. Ford claimed that if Nixon were to go to trial, it would take up too much of the nation's time, money, and attention. "I felt I had the obligation to spend 100 percent of my time on the problems of 230 million people rather than 25 percent of my time on the problems of one man," Ford explained.[2]

The American people might not have agreed. Ford ran for president in 1976 and lost to Democrat Jimmy Carter. Many people believe the Nixon pardon cost Ford enough votes to determine the election.

Richard Nixon retired to his San Clemente home. In 1980, he and Pat moved to Upper Saddle River, New Jersey. For the rest of his life he tried to rehabilitate his reputation. He wrote several books, and presidents of both parties sought his advice on foreign affairs.

Nixon died in April 1994. Some people did forgive him. They praised the government leader who opened relations with China, got the United States out of the Vietnam War, created a nuclear weapons treaty with the Soviet Union, and worked for peace in the Middle East.

To many others, Nixon's name still stood for Watergate. For them, Richard Nixon would always be responsible for what Gerald Ford called "our long national nightmare."[3]

☆ TIMELINE ☆

1969—*January 20*: Richard Milhous Nixon is inaugurated president.

1971—*June 13*: *The New York Times* begins publishing the Pentagon Papers, classified information about the Vietnam War.

1971—*September 3-4*: White House "Plumbers" break into office of Dr. Lewis Fielding, Daniel Ellsberg's psychiatrist.

1972—*March 30*: CRP Director John Mitchell approves Gemstone plan, including electronic surveillance of Democratic National Headquarters.

1972—*May 28*: A group directed by G. Gordon Liddy breaks into the Democratic headquarters at the Watergate on its third attempt.

1972—*June 17*: Police arrest five men breaking into the Watergate.

1972—*June 23*: Nixon and H. R. Haldeman discuss plans to have the CIA stop the FBI investigation of Watergate.

1972—*August 1*: *Washington Post* reveals a $25,000 check from President Nixon's campaign appeared in Watergate burglar Bernard Barker's bank account.

1972—*September 15*: A grand jury indicts the five Watergate burglars, E. Howard Hunt, and Liddy.

1972—*November 7*: Richard Nixon wins re-election by a landslide.

1973—*March 19*: Watergate burglar James McCord writes Judge John J. Sirica that Watergate defendants were under "political pressure" to keep silent.

1973—*March 21*: John Dean tells Nixon that there is "a cancer growing on the presidency," due to the hush money demands by Watergate defendants.

1973—*April 30*: Richard Nixon announces the resignations of H. R. Haldeman, John Ehrlichman, John Dean, and Attorney General Richard Kleindienst.

1973—*May 17*: Senate Watergate Committee begins hearings.

1973—*June 25–29*: Dean testifies before Senate Watergate Committee; Mentions "enemies list."

1973—*July 16*: Alexander Butterfield describes White House taping system.

1973—*July 23*: Special Prosecutor Archibald Cox subpoenas nine White House tapes; Nixon refuses to turn them over; Over the next several months Nixon will refuse many times to release tapes and other documents.

1973—*October 10*: Spiro Agnew resigns as vice president; A few days later Nixon nominates Gerald Ford to replace him.

1973—*October 20*: Attorney General Elliot Richardson resigns and deputy William Ruckelshaus are fired when they refuse to fire Cox; The Cox firing, which shocks the nation, is known as the "Saturday Night Massacre."

1973—*October 23*: Twenty-one Congress members introduce resolutions calling for Nixon's impeachment.

1974—*March 1*: Seven former Nixon aides are indicted for Watergate-related crimes; President Nixon is named an "unindicted co-conspirator."

1974—*April 29*: White House releases 1,308-page document that contains edited transcripts of presidential conversations.

1974—*May 9*: House Judiciary Committee opens impeachment proceedings.

1974—*July 24*: Supreme Court rules 8–0 that Nixon must turn over sixty-four tapes subpoenaed by Special Prosecutor Leon Jaworski.

1974—*July 27*: House Judiciary Committee approves first article of impeachment (obstruction of justice) by 27–11 vote.

1974—*August 5*: Nixon releases transcripts of June 23, 1972, "smoking pistol" conversation; Many former supporters leave him.

1974—*August 9*: Nixon resigns; Ford takes oath of office as thirty-eighth president.

1974—*September 8*: Ford issues Nixon a pardon for crimes he committed or might have committed as president.

☆ CHAPTER NOTES ☆

Chapter 1. "A Third-Rate Burglary Attempt"

1. E. Howard Hunt, *Undercover: Memoirs of an American Secret Agent* (New York: Berkley, 1974), p. 1.

2. James McCord, *A Piece of Tape*, quoted in David Wallechinsky and Irving Wallace, *The People's Almanac #2* (New York: Bantam, 1978), p. 99.

3. Hunt, p. 2.

4. Fred Emery, *Watergate: The Corruption of American Politics and the Fall of Richard Nixon* (New York: Simon & Schuster, 1995), p. 161.

Chapter 2. "I Had to Win"

1. Steve Tally, *Bland Ambition* (San Diego: Harcourt Brace Jovanovich, 1992), p. 296.

2. Ibid., p. 295.

3. *Chicago Daily News*, August 8, 1974, p. 6.

4. David Wallechinsky and Irving Wallace, *The People's Almanac* (Garden City, N.Y.: Doubleday, 1975), p. 318.

5. Stephen E. Ambrose, *Nixon: Education of a Politician* (New York: Simon & Schuster, 1987), p. 140.

6. Richard M. Nixon, *RN: The Memoirs of Richard Nixon* (New York: Grosset and Dunlap, 1978), p. 53.

7. David Halberstam, *The Fifties* (New York: Fawcett Columbine, 1993), p. 13.

8. Wallechinsky and Wallace, p. 319.

9. Ibid.

10. Richard M. Nixon, *Six Crises* (Garden City, N.Y.: Doubleday, 1962), p. 102.

11. Richard Nixon, "Checkers Speech, September 23, 1952," on *Great Speeches of the Twentieth Century*, Rhino Word Beat, 1993.

12. Ibid.

13. Wallechinsky and Wallace, p. 320.

14. Ibid., p. 321.

15. Tally, p. 312.

16. Ambrose, p. 571.

17. Gerald S. Strober and Deborah Hart Strober, *Nixon: An Oral History of His Presidency* (New York: HarperPerennial, 1994), p. 9.

18. Richard Nixon, "Postelection Press Conference, November 1962," on *Great Speeches of the Twentieth Century*, Rhino Word Beat, 1993.

19. Tally, p. 310.

20. Richard Nixon, "Postelection Press Conference," *Great Speeches*.

Chapter 3. "White House Horrors"

1. Fred Emery, *Watergate: The Corruption of American Politics and the Fall of Richard Nixon* (New York: Simon & Schuster, 1995), p. 180.

2. Ibid., p. 49.

3. Emery, p. 61.

4. Lewis Chester, Cal McCrystal, Stephen Aris, and William Showcross, *Watergate: The Full Inside Story* (New York: Ballantine, 1973), p. 16.

5. G. Gordon Liddy, *Will* (New York: St. Martin's, 1980), p. 193.

6. *New York Times* staff, *The Watergate Hearings: Break-in and Cover-up* (New York: Bantam, 1973), p. 836.

7. Gerald S. Strober and Deborah Hunt Strober, *Nixon: An Oral History of His Presidency* (New York: HarperPerennial, 1994), p. 273.

8. Emery, p. 99.

9. Chester et al., p. 98.

10. Emery, p. 96.

11. Ibid., p. 91.

12. Ibid., p. 94.

13. Chester et al., p. 142.

14. Liddy, p. 215.

15. Chester et al., p. 161.

Chapter 4. "A Cancer Growing on the Presidency"

1. Lewis Chester, Cal McCrystal, Stephen Aris, and William Shawcross, *Watergate: The Full Inside Story* (New York: Ballantine, 1973), p. 161.

2. Richard M. Nixon, *RN: The Memoirs of Richard Nixon* (New York: Grosset and Dunlap, 1978), p. 626.

3. Carl Bernstein and Bob Woodward, *All the President's Men* (New York: Warner, 1976), p. 24.

4. Ibid., p. 132.

5. Fred Emery, *Watergate: The Corruption of American Politics and the Fall of Richard Nixon* (New York: Simon & Schuster, 1995), p. 153.

6. Nixon, p. 640.

7. Chester et al., p. 183.

8. Ibid., p. 191.

9. Mercer Cross, ed., *Watergate: Chronology of a Crisis* (Washington, D.C.: Congressional Quarterly, 1973), p. 11.

10. Chester et al., p. 229.

11. Emery, p. 262.

12. Ibid., p. 274.

13. Nixon, p. 648.

14. Emery, p. 241.

15. Ibid., p. 353.

16. Chester et al., p. 246.

Chapter 5. America's Political Soap Opera

1. *New York Times* staff, *The Watergate Hearings: Break-in and Cover-up* (New York: Bantam, 1973), p. 44.

2. Sam J. Ervin, Jr., *The Whole Truth: The Watergate Conspiracy* (New York: Random House, 1980), p. 117.

3. Mercer Cross, ed., *Watergate: Chronology of a Crisis* (Washington, D.C.: Congressional Quarterly, 1973), p. 12.

4. *New York Times* staff, p. 9.

5. Cross, p. 64.

6. Ibid., p. 114.

7. Lewis Chester, Cal McCrystal, Stephen Aris, and William Shawcross, *Watergate: The Full Inside Story* (New York: Ballantine, 1973), p. 259.

8. Chester et al., p. 263.

9. Stephen E. Ambrose, *Nixon: Ruin and Recovery 1973–1990* (New York: Simon & Schuster, 1992), p. 201.

Chapter 6. "I Will Not Resign If Indicted!"

1. Paul F. Boller, Jr., *Presidential Campaigns* (New York: Oxford, 1984), p. 321.

2. Steve Tally, *Bland Ambition* (San Diego: Harcourt Brace Jovanovich, 1992), p. 338.

3. Boller, p. 324.

4. Gerald S. Strober and Deborah Hart Strober, *Nixon: An Oral History of His Presidency* (New York: HarperPerennial, 1994), p. 267.

5. Stephen E. Ambrose, *Nixon: Ruin and Recovery 1973–1990* (New York: Simon & Schuster, 1992), p. 223.

6. Fred Emery, *Watergate: The Corruption of American Politics and the Fall of Richard Nixon* (New York: Simon & Schuster, 1995), p. 383.

7. Tally, p. 343.

8. Ambrose, p. 339.

9. Ibid., p. 238.

Chapter 7. "Saturday Night Massacre"

1. Stephen E. Ambrose, *Nixon: Ruin and Recovery 1973–1990* (New York: Simon & Schuster, 1992), p. 233.

2. Gerald S. Strober and Deborah Hart Strober, *Nixon: An Oral History of His Presidency* (New York: HarperPerennial, 1994), p. 366.

3. Fred Emery, *Watergate: The Corruption of American Politics and the Fall of Richard Nixon* (New York: Simon & Schuster, 1995), p. 357.

4. Bob Woodward and Carl Bernstein, *The Final Days* (New York: Avon, 1976), p. 62.

5. Ibid., p. 314.

6. John J. Sirica, *To Set the Record Straight: The Break-In, The Tapes, The Conspirators, The Pardon* (New York: W. W. Norton, 1979), p. 152.

7. Ambrose, p. 247.

8. Ambrose, p. 249.

9. Ibid., p. 250.

Chapter 8. "Sinister Forces"

1. Fred Emery, *Watergate: The Corruption of American Politics and the Fall of Richard Nixon* (New York: Simon & Schuster, 1995), p. 411.

2. Stephen E. Ambrose, *Nixon: Ruin and Recovery 1973–1990* (New York: Simon & Schuster, 1992), p. 264.

3. Ibid., p. 277.

4. Richard M. Nixon, *RN: The Memoirs of Richard Nixon* (New York: Grosset and Dunlap, 1978), p. 950.

5. Richard Nixon, "November 7, 1973, Television Address," on *Great Speeches of the Twentieth Century*, Rhino Word Beat, 1993.

6. Ambrose, p. 298.

7. Ibid., p. 296.

8. Emery, p. 428.

9. John J. Sirica, *To Set the Record Straight: The Break-in, The Tapes, The Conspirators, The Pardon* (New York: W. W. Norton, 1979), p. 216.

10. Ambrose, p. 337.

11. Ibid., p. 332.

12. *Chicago Daily News*, August 8, 1974, p. 8.

13. Ambrose, p. 327.

14. Emery, p. 430.

15. David Halberstam, *The Powers That Be* (New York: Alfred A. Knopf, 1979), p. 700.

Chapter 9. "The Smoking Pistol"

1. David Wallechinsky and Irving Wallace, *The People's Almanac #2* (New York: Bantam, 1978), p. 98.

2. Bob Woodward and Carl Bernstein, *The Final Days* (New York: Avon, 1976), p. 254.

3. Fred Emery, *Watergate: The Corruption of American Politics and the Fall of Richard Nixon* (New York: Simon & Schuster, 1995), p. 445.

4. Woodward and Bernstein, p. 308.

5. Stephen E. Ambrose, *Nixon: Ruin and Recovery 1973–1990* (New York: Simon & Schuster, 1992), p. 384.

6. Leon Jaworski, *The Right and the Power: The Prosecution of Watergate* (New York: Reader's Digest, 1976), p. 204.

7. Woodward and Bernstein, p. 280.

8. Ambrose, p. 397.

9. *Chicago Daily News*, July 24, 1974, p. 13.

10. Woodward and Bernstein, p. 293.

11. *Chicago Daily News*, July 24, p. 13.

12. Ibid.

13. Woodward and Bernstein, p. 266.

14. Sam J. Ervin, Jr., *The Whole Truth: The Watergate Conspiracy* (New York: Random House, 1980), p. 284.

15. Woodward and Bernstein, p. 369.

16. Jaworski, p. 216.

17. Ambrose, p. 410.

18. *Chicago Daily News*, August 8, 1974, p. 10.

19. Emery, p. 474.

20. *Chicago Daily News*, August 8, 1974, p. 1.

21. Emery, p. 478.

22. Richard Nixon, "Resignation Speech, August 8, 1974," on *Great Speeches of the Twentieth Century*, Rhino Word Beat, 1993.

23. *Chicago Tribune*, August 9, 1974, p. 10.

24. John J. Sirica, *To Set the Record Straight: The Break-in, The Tapes, The Conspirators, The Pardon* (New York: W. W. Norton, 1979), p. 230.

25. Woodward and Bernstein, p. 455.

Chapter 10. "Our Long National Nightmare"

1. Stephen E. Ambrose, *Nixon: Ruin and Recovery 1973–1990* (New York: Simon & Schuster, 1992), p. 405.

2. Gerald S. Strober and Deborah Hart Strober, *Nixon: An Oral History of His Presidency* (New York: HarperPerennial, 1994), p. 486.

3. Fred Emery, *Watergate: The Corruption of American Politics and the Fall of Richard Nixon* (New York: Simon & Schuster, 1995), p. 482.

☆ FURTHER READING ☆

Ambrose, Stephen E. *Nixon: Education of a Politician.* New York: Simon & Schuster, 1987.

———. *Nixon: Ruin and Recovery 1973–1990.* New York: Simon & Schuster, 1992.

Bernstein, Carl, and Bob Woodward. *All the President's Men.* New York: Warner, 1976.

———. *The Final Days.* New York: Avon, 1976.

Chester, Lewis, Cal McCrystal, Stephen Aris, and William Shawcross. *Watergate: The Full Inside Story.* New York: Ballantine, 1973.

Emery, Fred. *Watergate: The Corruption of American Politics and the Fall of Richard Nixon.* New York: Simon & Schuster, 1995.

Haldeman, H. R. *The Haldeman Diaries: Inside the Nixon White House.* New York: Berkley, 1995.

Herda, D. J. *United States v. Nixon: Watergate and the President.* Springfield, N.J.: Enslow Publishers, Inc., 1996.

Jaworski, Leon. *The Right and the Power: The Prosecution of Watergate.* New York: Reader's Digest, 1976.

Liddy, G. Gordon. *Will.* New York: St. Martin's, 1980.

Nixon, Richard M. *RN: The Memoirs of Richard Nixon.* New York: Grosset and Dunlap, 1978.

Sirica, John J. *To Set the Record Straight: The Break-in, The Tapes, The Conspirators, The Pardon.* New York: W. W. Norton, 1979.

Strober, Gerald S., and Deborah Hart Strober. *Nixon: An Oral History of His Presidency.* New York: HarperPerennial, 1994.

White, Theodore. *The Making of the President 1972.* New York: Bantam, 1973.

☆ INDEX ☆